MW00979222

Best Recipes from The Weekly

Food Editor Pamela Clark says: Here at last is a collection of the most popular recipes from The Weekly's Test Kitchen – everything from pikelets and rock cakes to sumptuous dinner party desserts; recipes to suit all tastes and all seasons.

Editor
Pamela Clark

Art Director
Robbylee Phelan

Photographer
Russell Brooks

Home Economists
Barbara Northwood
Agnes Lee
Laura Robertson
Lucy Clayton
Elizabeth Carden

Food Stylist
Jacqui Hing

Editor's Assistant
Evelyn Follers

Cover photographed at Country Form Pty Ltd, Sydney.
Inside front cover: Cutlets Wellington; Lamb Curry; Stuffed Loin of Lamb; Ratatouille Lamb (recipes P52, 53).
Inside back cover: Apricot and Honey Rock Cakes; Mixed Fruit Rock Cakes; Currant and Lemon Pikelets (recipes P87).

ISBN 0 949892 21 1

Typeset by Photoset Computer Service Pty Ltd, Sydney, Australia
Printed by Dai Nippon Co Ltd, Tokyo, Japan
Published by Australian Consolidated Press, 54 Park Street, Sydney
Distributed by Network Distribution Company, 54 Park Street, Sydney

CONTENTS

OVEN TEMPERATURES

Electric Temperatures

	Celsius	Fahrenheit
Very slow	120	250
Slow	150	300
Moderately slow	160-180	325-350
Moderate	190-200	375-400
Moderately hot	220-230	425-450
Hot	250-260	475-500
Very hot	270-290	525-550

Gas Temperatures	Celsius	Fahrenheit
Very slow	120	250
Slow	140-150	275-300
Moderately slow	160	325
Moderate	180	350
Moderately hot	190	375
Hot	200-230	400-450
Very hot	250-260	475-500

CUP MEASURES

	Metric	Imperial
1 cup flour	155g	5oz
1 cup sugar (crystal or castor)	250g	8oz
1 cup brown sugar, firmly packed	185g	6oz
1 cup icing sugar, sifted	185g	6oz
1 cup butter	250g	8oz
1 cup honey, golden syrup, treacle	375g	12oz
1 cup fresh breadcrumbs	60g	2 oz
1 cup packaged dry breadcrumbs	155g	5oz
1 cup crushed biscuit crumbs	125g	4oz
1 cup rice, uncooked	220g	7oz
1 cup mixed fruit or individual fruit, such as sultanas	185g	6oz
1 cup nuts, chopped	125g	4oz
1 coconut, desiccated	90g	3oz

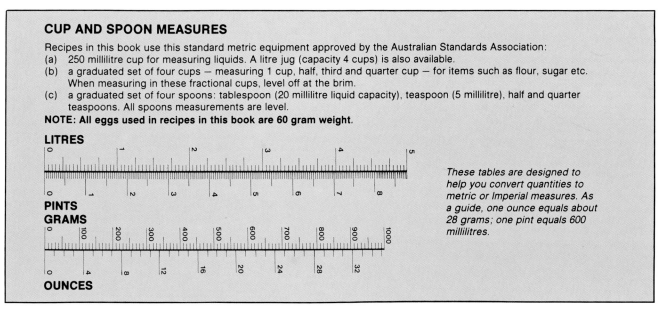

CUP AND SPOON MEASURES

Recipes in this book use this standard metric equipment approved by the Australian Standards Association:
(a)   250 millilitre cup for measuring liquids. A litre jug (capacity 4 cups) is also available.
(b)   a graduated set of four cups — measuring 1 cup, half, third and quarter cup — for items such as flour, sugar etc. When measuring in these fractional cups, level off at the brim.
(c)   a graduated set of four spoons: tablespoon (20 millilitre liquid capacity), teaspoon (5 millilitre), half and quarter teaspoons. All spoons measurements are level.

NOTE: All eggs used in recipes in this book are 60 gram weight.

LITRES

PINTS
GRAMS

These tables are designed to help you convert quantities to metric or Imperial measures. As a guide, one ounce equals about 28 grams; one pint equals 600 millilitres.

OUNCES

Terrines are a relative of the pate, but usually with a coarser, denser texture, making them more satisfying to serve for a main course. Terrines benefit in flavor by being kept refrigerated for at least 24 hours before serving. They will keep for up to a week, but do not freeze well.

PORK AND CHICKEN TERRINE
250g bacon
250g veal steak
125g pork fillet
125g chicken fillet
3 bay leaves
2 large onions
2 cloves garlic
125g pistachio nuts
1 egg
1 tablespoon canned green
   peppercorns
2 tablespoons brandy
1 teaspoon dried basil
1 tablespoon chopped parsley
salt, pepper
2 slices ham

Remove rind from bacon. Place bay leaves at base of loaf tin (base measures 9cm × 22cm). Line tin with bacon rashers, reserve enough bacon to cover top.

Mince veal in food processor until fine. Place in bowl, process chicken and pork, add to veal. Process onions and garlic, add to minced meats.

Shell nuts, add to meat mixture. Add egg, peppercorns, brandy, basil, chopped parsley, salt and pepper to meat mixture, mix until well combined. Spread half of mixture in bacon-lined loaf tin. Cut ham into thin strips. Layer on top of minced meats, spread remaining mixture on top of ham slices. Lay reserved bacon slices on top, cover with aluminium foil, bake in moderate oven 1½ hours, cool. Refrigerate overnight.

From left: Pork and Chicken Terrine; Herbed Pork and Spinach Terrine; Layered Vegetable Terrine.

TERRINES
& PATES

HERBED PORK AND SPINACH TERRINE

This recipe comes from Zita's restaurant in Melbourne, which is renowned for its pates and terrines.

3 bunches spinach (about 20 leaves)
750g pork mince
500g lean bacon
⅓ cup chopped parsley
¼ clove garlic
4 teaspoons chopped fresh basil or
  1 teaspoon dried
1 teaspoon thyme
1 teaspoon nutmeg
1 teaspoon pepper
1 teaspoon salt
3 medium onions
30g butter
250g chicken livers
¼ cup brandy
⅓ cup madeira
⅓ cup cream
4 eggs
60g pistachio nuts
2 thin slices ham
60g thinly sliced speck (smoked bacon)

Remove stalks from spinach, wash spinach leaves, tear up roughly, place in steamer or large pan. Cover tightly, cook until leaves are tender. Drain, press out all moisture. Place spinach in food processor, process until spinach is finely chopped. Place spinach in bowl, add mince, 125g finely chopped bacon, chopped parsley, crushed garlic, basil, thyme, nutmeg, pepper and salt. Cover chicken livers with water, leave 30 minutes.

Melt butter in pan, add finely chopped onions. Cook until onions are just tender. Drain chicken livers, clean, cut livers into 1cm pieces. Add livers to pan, cook 2 minutes. Pour brandy over, mix well, stir in madeira and cream. Bring mixture to boil, remove from heat, allow to cool then stir into spinach mixture with lightly beaten eggs, mix well. Shell pistachio nuts, cover pistachio nuts with hot water, leave 5 minutes, remove skins.

Add nuts to mixture, mix well. Line base and sides of loaf tin (base measures 12cm × 22cm) with bacon (remove rind first). Add half the spinach mixture to tin, make a furrow in centre of spinach mixture; place speck on top of ham slices, roll up, place ham rolls along furrow. Spoon remaining spinach mixture on top. Cover with remaining bacon. Cover with aluminium foil, secure with string, place in baking dish with hot water to come halfway up sides of loaf tin; bake in moderate oven for 1½ hours. Remove from oven, place a weight on top, cool, refrigerate overnight.

LAYERED VEGETABLE TERRINE

This superb terrine, with its layers of colorful, crunchy vegetables and creamy chicken mousse, is a speciality of the Lygon Arms in Broadway, Worcestershire, England. Our thanks to Douglas Barrington, Australian-born managing director of the Lygon Arms, for this recipe.

250g zucchini
250g carrots
250g broccoli
250g bacon
2 chicken fillets
2 egg whites
300ml carton cream
TOMATO SAUCE
750g ripe tomatoes
1 tablespoon chopped mint
1 clove garlic
½ cup water
salt, pepper
½ teaspoon sugar

Remove ends from zucchini and cut into thin slices lengthwise. Peel carrots and cut away ends and tips, cut into thin slices lengthwise. Wash broccoli and cut into small flowerets. Place carrots in pan of boiling water, cook 3 minutes; drain and rinse under cold running water. Repeat process with broccoli. Place zucchini in boiling water, cook 1 minute; drain and rinse under cold running water.

Remove rind from bacon, chop bacon roughly. Cut chicken fillets into large pieces. Place bacon and chicken in food processor and process until finely minced. While motor is running, pour egg whites through funnel and process 30 seconds. Slowly add cream, process until just combined.

Spread small amount of chicken mousse over base of greased ovenproof dish or loaf tin (base measures 9cm × 22cm). Arrange a layer of carrots over mousse. Spread another thin layer of mousse on top of carrots, arrange a layer of zucchini on top. Repeat process with carrots and end with a layer of broccoli. Spread remaining mousse over broccoli. Cover top with a sheet of aluminium foil, place in a baking dish with hot water half-way up the sides. Bake in a slow oven 50 minutes. Remove dish from water and cool 15 minutes before turning out. Cut into slices, serve with Tomato Sauce.

Tomato Sauce: Cut tomatoes into quarters. Place tomatoes, mint, crushed garlic and water in pan, bring to boil, reduce heat, simmer 20 minutes. Place tomatoes in blender and blend on high speed 30 seconds. Push mixture through strainer, season with salt and pepper, add sugar.

VEAL PEPPERCORN TERRINE WITH ORANGE SAUCE

This terrine is at its best after being refrigerated for 48 hours. It can be made and refrigerated a week before it is needed. The Orange Sauce can also be made at the same time as the Terrine.

500g veal steak
250g ham
500g ham fat
250g chicken livers
1 tablespoon brandy
3 bay leaves or celery leaves
1 tablespoon canned green
   peppercorns
1 onion
1 clove garlic
30g butter
2 eggs
¼ teaspoon thyme
¼ cup chopped parsley
salt, pepper

ORANGE SAUCE
1 lemon
1 cup seville orange marmalade (or
   any bitter marmalade)
2 tablespoons port
½ teaspoon dry mustard
½ teaspoon french mustard
¼ cup water

Place veal, ham and a quarter of the ham fat in food processor, process in batches until finely minced. Place chicken livers in bowl, add brandy; stand 30 minutes. Process livers until fine, add to veal mixture. Slice remaining fat thinly, arrange bay or celery leaves over base of 20cm × 10cm ovenproof dish or loaf tin, place a layer of ham fat over base and sides (carefully covering leaves).

Add peppercorns to veal mixture. Saute chopped onion and crushed garlic in butter, add to veal mixture with eggs, thyme, parsley, salt and pepper; mix well. Place veal mixture

on top of ham fat, press down firmly, top with remaining slices of ham fat. Cover tightly with aluminium foil, place in baking dish with hot water halfway up the sides.

Bake in moderately slow oven 1½ hours. Remove dish from water, cool slightly, place chopping board on top of terrine, then weight with a brick or something heavy. When cold, refrigerate until required.

Orange Sauce: Remove rind from lemon using vegetable peeler, cut rind into thin strips 5cm in length. Place rind in pan of boiling water, simmer 5 minutes, strain. Heat marmalade in pan until melted, push through sieve; discard orange pieces and return marmalade to pan. Add port, mustards, 1 tablespoon lemon juice, water and rind, cook over low heat 10 minutes, uncovered.

Serve warm over cold terrine.

All of these delicious pate recipes can be made in a blender or food processor, or ingredients can be pushed through a sieve. They can all be made the day before required, covered and refrigerated. Serve with hot toast, crackers or Melba toast. A variety of salad vegetables can be served with the pates.

GRAND MARNIER PATE
500g chicken livers
⅓ cup Grand Marnier
90g butter
1 small onion
1 clove garlic
⅓ cup cream
salt, pepper
¼ teaspoon nutmeg
½ teaspoon thyme

Trim livers and cut in half. Place in bowl, cover with Grand Marnier and allow to stand 2 hours. Strain livers, reserve liquid. Melt half the butter in pan, add chopped onion, crushed garlic and livers, cook 3 minutes over moderate heat, add .Grand Marnier liquid and cook further 1 minute. Remove from heat and puree liver mixture in blender or food processor. Melt remaining butter and add to livers; mix thoroughly. Add cream and stir through, season with salt, pepper, nutmeg and thyme. Place in serving dish and refrigerate overnight.
Serves 4.

SMOKED OYSTER PATE
30g butter
2 rashers bacon
½ teaspoon chopped basil
125g packaged cream cheese
½ teaspoon worcestershire sauce
1 tablespoon dry sherry
½ teaspoon lemon juice
salt, pepper
100g can smoked oyster spread

Heat butter in pan, add finely chopped bacon and finely chopped basil, cook until bacon is tender. Drain. Put bacon in blender or food processor, blend until fine. Add cream cheese, worcestershire sauce, sherry, lemon juice, salt and pepper. Blend until smooth. Add smoked oyster spread, blend until well combined. Spoon into serving dish, refrigerate overnight.
Serves 4.

SMOKED EEL PATE
1kg smoked eel
60g butter
60g packaged cream cheese
1 tablespoon lemon juice
1 tablespoon cream
salt, pepper

Remove skin from eel, scrape flesh from bones, place flesh in food processor or blender, process or blend until smooth, add soft butter and cream cheese, then lemon juice and cream, process until smooth. Season with salt and pepper. Place in serving dish. Refrigerate overnight.
Serves 4.

PATE OF PESTO
½ cup (90g) pinenuts
1 large bunch basil (about 4 cups loosely packed leaves)
1 clove garlic
salt, pepper
⅓ cup oil
500g ricotta cheese
⅓ cup grated parmesan cheese

Place pinenuts on baking tray, bake in moderate oven 5 minutes or until light golden brown, cool. Place basil leaves in food processor with peeled garlic, 2 tablespoons of the pinenuts, salt and pepper. Process until mixture is finely chopped. With processor still going add oil in a thin stream. Process a further 1 second, until the mixture forms a smooth paste.

(Blender can also be used; stop blender and scrape the mixture down sides occasionally to mix evenly).

Combine ricotta cheese and parmesan cheese in small bowl of electric mixer, beat on medium speed until mixture is smooth. Combine cheese mixture with basil mixture, mix well. Spoon mixture into mould (or 4 small individual moulds) which has been lined with a piece of cheesecloth. Fold overhanging sides of cheesecloth over pate, press top down with palm of hand. Refrigerate overnight. Gently lift pate out of mould, turn on to serving plate and carefully peel off cheesecloth. Press remaining roughly chopped pinenuts over top and sides of pate.
Serves 4.

SALMON PATE
220g can red salmon
125g packaged cream cheese
½ cup mayonnaise
salt, pepper
2 tablespoons lime or lemon juice
125g butter

Combine drained salmon, softened cream cheese, mayonnaise, salt, pepper and lemon juice in blender or food processor. Add melted butter, blend until smooth. Spoon salmon mixture into serving dish, refrigerate until set.
Serves 4.

MELBA TOAST
Melba Toast is an ideal accompaniment to pates or terrines. It is simple to make and will keep for months in an airtight container.

To make it, take a square loaf of white unsliced bread, trim away all crusts. Cut loaf in half to make it easy to handle, then cut each half through diagonally. Place widest side of each piece on board and use sharp or electric knife to cut slices as thinly as possible.

Place triangles on ungreased flat oven trays, bake in moderate oven about 20 minutes, or until bread is golden brown, curled and crisp. It must be completely dried out, or it will develop mould during storing. Cool before storing in airtight container.

Top, from left: Grand Marnier Pate, Smoked Oyster Pate, Smoked Eel Pate. Middle: Salmon Pate. Front: Pate of Pesto.

SOUPS

Cold soups make a great first course during the hot weather. The recipes we have chosen are speedy to make. We have also made use of convenience foods. The soups are best made the day before serving to allow flavors to develop and the soup to be thoroughly chilled.

PUMPKIN SOUP
500g pumpkin
2 onions
1 carrot
3½ cups chicken stock
¼ teaspoon nutmeg
salt, pepper

Peel pumpkin, onions and carrot; cut into pieces. Put all vegetables in pan. Add chicken stock and nutmeg, salt and pepper. Bring to boil; reduce heat, simmer covered until pumpkin is tender. Puree in blender or food processor, or rub through sieve. Chill. Serve with spoonful of sour cream and chopped chives.

Serves 4.

CURRIED ZUCCHINI SOUP
1 onion
30g butter
2 teaspoons curry powder
1 clove garlic
500g zucchini
1 tablespoon lemon juice
salt, pepper
2½ cups chicken stock
⅔ cup cream

Coarsely chop onion; melt butter in pan, add onion, curry powder and crushed garlic. Cook, stirring few minutes or until onion is transparent, place mixture into blender or food processor with roughly chopped zucchini, lemon juice and about half the stock. Blend or process until vegetables are finely chopped. Stir in remaining stock and cream, cover, refrigerate for several hours. Push through fine strainer, discard vegetable pulp, season with salt and pepper; refrigerate before serving.

Serves 4.

BEEF AND VEGETABLE CONSOMME
430g can beef consomme
1¾ cups water
¾ cup orange juice
2 carrots
2 zucchini

Place consomme in pan, add water and strained orange juice, bring to boil; reduce heat, simmer uncovered 2 minutes. Cut carrots and zucchini into thin strips. Bring pan of water to boil, add carrots and zucchini, cook, uncovered, 2 minutes; drain, rinse under cold running water. Add vegetables to soup. Refrigerate covered until chilled.

Serves 6.

CORN AND BACON SOUP
425g can creamed corn
2 cups chicken stock
30g butter
½ green pepper
4 shallots
1 bacon rasher
¾ cup cream

Combine creamed corn and chicken stock, heat gently. Melt butter in pan, add chopped pepper, chopped shallots and finely chopped bacon, cook until bacon is crisp. Puree pepper, shallots and bacon in blender. Add corn mixture and blend until smooth. Cool, stir in cream. Refrigerate until well chilled. Garnish with finely chopped shallots.

Serves 4.

QUICK GAZPACHO
1 small cucumber
1 small onion
1 red pepper
2 sticks celery
1 small chilli
400g can tomatoes
½ cup bottled french dressing
½ cup water
salt, pepper
2 tablespoons chopped parsley

Peel cucumber and onion, chop roughly; chop pepper and celery roughly; seed chilli. Place vegetables in blender or food processor with undrained tomatoes, french dressing and water, blend or process until vegetables are finely chopped. Season with salt and pepper, cover, refrigerate several hours. Stir in parsley.

Serves 4.

At back, from left: Pumpkin Soup; Curried Zucchini Soup; Beef and Vegetable Consomme.
At front, from left: Corn and Bacon Soup; Quick Gazpacho.

Here are three quick and easy soups to make, and three which take a little longer to prepare. Make a main meal out of the Hearty Winter Soup or Mulligatawny by serving with hot crusty bread.

HEARTY WINTER SOUP

This soup has a delicious variety of winter vegetables combined in a rich lamb shank stock with lentils. Cook the stock for the soup a couple of days before required and add most of the vegetables on the day of serving. Stir the colorful pepper and parsley in as you serve the soup.
Make a complete meal by serving with hot crusty bread.

3 lamb shanks
2½ litres water
1 onion
1 stick celery
½ cup brown lentils
4 carrots
2 potatoes
1 small turnip
¼ small cabbage
2 rashers bacon
1 onion, extra
1 stick celery, extra
2 beef stock cubes
2 tablespoons chopped parsley
¼ chopped red pepper
salt, pepper

Add lamb shanks to water in pan, add roughly chopped onion and celery, salt and pepper. Cover, simmer 1½ hours, cool, refrigerate overnight. Cover lentils with water, soak overnight.

Next day, strain stock, discard fat and vegetables. Return stock to pan with drained lentils and chopped meat from shanks. Bring to boil, add chopped carrots, potatoes, turnip and shredded cabbage. Remove rind from bacon, cook chopped bacon, extra onion and extra celery until onion is transparent, in separate pan; add to soup with crumbled stock cubes. Simmer, covered, for one hour. Add parsley and red pepper just before serving. Season with salt and pepper.
Serves 6 to 8.

CURRIED CREAM OF VEGETABLE SOUP
30g butter
2 leeks
250g zucchini
1 clove garlic
1 stick celery
4 sprigs parsley
1 teaspoon curry powder
2 medium potatoes
1 litre chicken stock
salt, pepper
⅓ cup cream

Melt butter in large pan, add sliced leeks, sliced zucchini, crushed garlic, chopped celery, parsley and curry powder; cook 5 minutes, stirring occasionally. Chop potatoes into large dice, add to pan. Add chicken stock, bring to boil, reduce heat, simmer covered 30 minutes. Puree in blender or food processor in batches, or push through sieve. Return soup to saucepan, season with salt and pepper, stir in cream and reheat without boiling.
Serves 4.

CREAMY SCALLOP SOUP
2 fish fillets
3 cups water
¼ cup dry white wine
salt, pepper
375g scallops
60g butter
6 shallots
125g mushrooms
1 tablespoon chopped parsley
½ cup cream

Remove skin and bones from fish, place in pan with water, wine, salt and pepper; bring to boil. Reduce heat, cover, simmer 25 minutes. Strain through sieve, reserve fish and stock. Heat butter in pan, add chopped shallots and sliced mushrooms, cook 1 minute. Add reserved stock, fish which has been broken into small pieces and parsley; simmer 10 to 15 minutes. Add cream and halved scallops, heat without boiling.
Serves 4 to 6.

At back from left: Hearty Winter Soup; Curried Cream of Vegetable Soup; Creamy Scallop Soup.

At front from left: Salmon Asparagus Soup; Chinese Broccoli and Chicken Soup; Mulligatawny.

MULLIGATAWNY

An Indian curry flavored soup. The name comes from two Tamil words: molegoo (pepper) and tunee (water).

¼ cup red lentils
1kg chicken thighs
1¾ litres (7 cups) water
1 teaspoon salt
60g butter
1 onion
2 cloves garlic
½ teaspoon grated green ginger
1 tablespoon curry powder
½ teaspoon garam masala
¼ teaspoon chilli powder
pinch cinnamon
2 tablespoons flour
2 tomatoes
2 chicken stock cubes
1 tablespoon tomato paste
1 green pepper
2 sticks celery
1 carrot
salt, pepper
283ml can coconut milk
cooked rice

Pour enough hot water over lentils to cover well, put aside. Place chicken in pan, with water and salt. Bring to boil; reduce heat, simmer covered 1¼ hours, remove and reserve chicken, allow stock to become cold, remove fat from stock.

Melt butter in large pan, add chopped onion, cook until transparent. Add ginger and crushed garlic, cook 1 minute more. Add curry powder, chilli powder, garam masala and cinnamon, stir over low heat 2 minutes.

Add flour to pan, stir over low heat 1 minute. Stir in peeled and chopped tomatoes, reserved stock, tomato paste, crumbled stock cubes and drained lentils. Bring to boil; add sliced pepper, sliced carrot and chopped celery. Reduce heat, simmer uncovered 15 minutes, cover pan, simmer 30 minutes or until vegetables are tender. Season with salt and pepper.

Push vegetables with liquid through sieve, or puree in blender or food processor (do this in several batches). Return soup to pan, bring to boil, reduce heat, stir in coconut milk and shredded meat from chicken thighs. Sprinkle a spoonful of cooked rice on top of each bowl of soup. You'll need to cook about ½ cup of rice. Serve the soup with papadams, if desired; fry as directed on packet.

Serves 6.

SALMON ASPARAGUS SOUP

440g can cream of asparagus soup
220g can red salmon
1 cup water
300ml carton cream
salt, pepper
2 tablespoons chopped chives

Drain salmon, remove skin and bones. Puree salmon in food processor or blender. Combine with undiluted soup and water in pan, mix well. Reserve 2 tablespoons of the cream for garnishing, add remaining cream to soup, heat without boiling. Season with salt and pepper. Pour soup into serving dishes, swirl 2 teaspoons of cream on top of each, sprinkle with chopped chives.

Serves 4.

CHINESE BROCCOLI AND CHICKEN SOUP

1 whole chicken breast
2cm piece green ginger
2 litres water
salt, pepper
½ teaspoon sugar
1 teaspoon cornflour
2 slices ham
190g can champignons
375g broccoli
3 teaspoons soy sauce
1½ tablespoons cornflour, extra
2 tablespoons water, extra

Remove skin from chicken breast, cut meat from breast bones. Place bones, peeled and thinly sliced ginger and water in pan, bring to boil, reduce heat, simmer covered 20 minutes. Discard bones. Cut meat from breast into fine strips, combine with salt, sugar and cornflour, mix well. Cut ham into narrow strips, drain and slice champignons. Cut broccoli into small flowerets, put in another pan with enough boiling salted water to cover; boil 1 minute, drain, rinse under cold water, drain again.

Add meat and ham to stock, stir to separate strips. Boil uncovered 5 minutes. Add broccoli and champignons and stir in blended soy sauce, extra cornflour and extra water. Stir until boiling, season with salt and pepper.

Serves 6.

ENTREES

Most of the entrees we have chosen are quick and easy to assemble and serve, but still look elegant and taste wonderful.

SEAFOOD WITH SMOKED SALMON CREAM

Prepare sauce up to three hours before serving.

250g scallops
250g cooked prawns
8 oysters
2 shallots
salt, pepper
2 cups water
30g butter
2 tablespoons plain flour
2 slices smoked salmon
¼ cup cream
2 tablespoons dry white wine
1 teaspoon lemon juice
2 tablespoons chopped chives

Clean scallops, place in pan with water, chopped shallots, salt and pepper. Bring to boil, reduce heat, simmer 1 minute. Strain scallops, reserve stock, remove shallots.

Measure 1½ cups of reserved stock. Heat butter in pan, add flour, stir over heat 1 minute. Gradually add reserved stock, wine and lemon juice, stir over heat until mixture boils and thickens. Place roughly chopped salmon in blender or food processor, add cream, blend until smooth.

Add salmon mixture to sauce, mix well; season with salt and pepper, spoon hot sauce over scallops, shelled prawns and oysters, sprinkle with chopped chives.
Serves 4.

PROSCIUTTO AND PAPAW

Prosciutto is Italian raw ham; if un-available, substitute slices of leg ham.

1 papaw
4 slices prosciutto
½ red pepper
½ green pepper
¼ cup oil
2 tablespoons dry white wine
salt, pepper
½ clove garlic

Cut papaw in quarters, remove seeds. Arrange a slice of prosciutto over each quarter of papaw. Slice peppers thinly, put into bowl. Put oil, wine, salt, crushed garlic and pepper in screw-top jar; shake well. Pour dressing over peppers; mix well. Arrange peppers with dressing over papaw and pro-sciutto. Refrigerate until ready to serve.

Serves 4.

SEAFOOD WITH MANGO

1 avocado
1 mango
10 cooked king prawns
¼ cup bottled french dressing
2 tablespoons lemon juice
2 tablespoons mayonnaise
2 teaspoons mild chilli sauce
pepper
1 tablespoon chopped chives
curly endive

Cut avocado in half, remove stone; peel and slice avocado; peel and slice mango; shell and devein prawns. Combine avocado, mango and prawns, pour over combined french dressing and lemon juice. Season with pepper, stand 10 minutes. Combine mayonnaise and chilli sauce, drain dressing from prawn mixture into may-onnaise mixture, mix well. Pour dress-ing over prawn and fruit mixture. Re-frigerate until ready to serve. Serve with curly endive, sprinkle with chopped chives.

Serves 4.

AVOCADO SALAD

Use the lettuce of your choice or a mixture. The red-leafed Italian radicchio and mignonette would look attractive with endive.

1 lettuce
1 pepper (red, green or yellow)
3 sticks celery
2 avocados
½ cup oil
1 teaspoon walnut oil
1 clove garlic
1 egg
1 tablespoon white vinegar
1 tablespoon lemon juice
¼ teaspoon worcestershire sauce
few drops tabasco
salt, pepper

Wash lettuce, pat dry. Put into plastic bag, refrigerate until crisp. Make dressing by combining oils and crushed garlic. Allow to stand for approximately 1 hour. Discard garlic. Coddle egg by placing it in hot water for 1 minute. Blend egg in blender till well mixed. Gradually beat in the garlic-flavoured oil. Continue beating while adding the vinegar, lemon juice, worcestershire sauce, tabasco, salt and pepper. Refrigerate until serving time. Tear lettuce into pieces, slice pepper and celery and combine in a large salad bowl. Add peeled, sliced avocados, serve with the dressing.
Serves 4.

SEAFOOD COCKTAIL SAUCE

Try this sauce, or one of the two on the opposite page, over fresh oysters or any seafood.

2 egg yolks
90g butter
2 teaspoons lemon juice
½ teaspoon tabasco
2 teaspoons tomato paste
2 tablespoons cream

Combine in top of double saucepan egg yolks, butter and lemon juice. Stir over simmering water until sauce has thickened. Remove from heat, stir in tabasco and tomato paste, mix well, stir in cream, pour sauce into small bowl, cover with plastic wrap, cool to room temperature. Do not refrigerate or butter will set firmly.
Makes approximately ⅔ cup.

SPINACH PARCELS WITH SEAFOOD

Prepare and refrigerate Spinach Parcels the day before required. Prepare stock for Sauce several hours before, complete Sauce as close to serving time as possible.

125g feta cheese
30g stuffed olives
1 tomato
2 tablespoons sour cream
pepper
spinach leaves
15g butter
SEAFOOD SAUCE
500g green prawns
2 cups water
⅓ cup cream
1 egg yolk
salt, pepper

Cut feta cheese into small cubes; combine with finely chopped olives, peeled and chopped tomato, sour cream and pepper, mix well. Cook spinach leaves in boiling water 1 minute, drain, cut away stalks. Pat leaves dry with absorbent paper. Divide cheese mixture evenly between spinach leaves down centre at one end. Roll up, enclosing ends. Place rolls in ovenproof dish, dot with butter, cover, bake in moderately hot oven 15 minutes until heated through. Top with Seafood Sauce.

Seafood Sauce: Shell and devein prawns, reserve shells. Place shells and water into pan, bring to boil, reduce heat, simmer covered 15 minutes. Strain stock through fine sieve. Return stock to pan, bring to boil, add prawns, cook until just tender, about 2 minutes, drain immediately, reserving ½ cup of the stock. Place reserved stock, cream and egg yolk into pan, stir over low heat until sauce thickens, do not boil. Add prawns, mix well, season with salt and pepper.

Serves 4.

ANCHOVY SAUCE

1 cup mayonnaise
1 clove garlic
45g can anchovy fillets
1 tablespoon chopped parsley
1 tablespoon tomato sauce

Combine finely chopped anchovy fillets, crushed garlic and other ingredients.

TARTARE SAUCE

½ cup mayonnaise
1½ tablespoons sour cream
2 teaspoons chopped fresh dill
1 teaspoon chopped chives
2 teaspoons chopped parsley
1 teaspoon capers
3 shallots
1 teaspoon lemon juice
salt, pepper

Finely chop shallots and capers; combine all ingredients.

SAVORIES

Choose a selection of these savories to serve with drinks. Most can be prepared ahead; some require last minute cooking.

SMOKED EEL AND CHIVE SPREAD

Make the spread the day before required for the best flavor.

90g butter
185g smoked eel
½ x 300g carton sour cream
1 tablespoon mayonnaise
1 tablespoon lemon juice
½ teaspoon worcestershire sauce
1 tablespoon finely chopped chives

Combine butter and skinned, boned eel in food processor or blender; blend until smooth. Add sour cream, mayonnaise, lemon juice and worcestershire sauce, beat well. Push through sieve. Stir in half the chives. Spread on rounds of buttered pumpernickel or rye bread or serve with crackers. Sprinkle with remaining chives.

CHICKEN WINGS WITH SHALLOTS

These are best marinated overnight. Be careful; they spatter when frying.

1kg chicken wings
½ cup cornflour
½ cup soy sauce
¼ cup sugar
10 shallots
oil for deep frying

Wash and dry chicken wings. Cut off wing tips at joint. (Use wing tips in another dish or to make soup.) Cut rest of the wings at joint to give two pieces. In large bowl, combine cornflour, soy sauce and sugar, mix well until sugar is dissolved. Add chopped shallots and wings, stand for 3 hours or cover and refrigerate overnight, turn occasionally. Deep fry in hot oil until golden brown. Drain on absorbent paper.

MINI FLAKY PIZZAS

Prepare these on their trays several hours before required. Bake just before serving.

2 sheets ready-rolled puff pastry
2 tablespoons tomato paste, approximately
60g sliced salami
3 tomatoes
250g mozzarella cheese
60g stuffed olives
45g can anchovy fillets
dried basil

Use 8cm cutter to cut nine rounds from each sheet of pastry. Place pastry rounds on oven trays. Spread each round lightly with tomato paste. Top each with salami slice, then a slice of peeled tomato. Sprinkle lightly with basil. Sprinkle with grated mozzarella, top with sliced olives and drained, chopped anchovies. Bake in moderately hot oven 10 to 15 minutes, or until well browned. Place on wire rack to cool 5 minutes before serving.
Makes 18.

MEXICAN MEAT TURNOVERS

250g minced steak
1 small onion
1 clove garlic
pinch chilli powder
1 small green pepper
½ x 400g can tomatoes
1 tablespoon tomato paste
¼ cup water
1 beef stock cube
½ x 310g can red kidney beans
salt, pepper
2 x 375g packets puff pastry
1 egg for glazing
oil for deep-frying

Add meat to pan, stir over high heat until meat is well browned, mashing with fork to break up lumps. Add finely chopped onion, cook until tender.

Add crushed garlic and chilli powder to pan, cook 1 minute. Add sliced pepper and undrained mashed tomatoes, mix well. Stir in water, crumbled stock cube, tomato paste, salt and pepper. Bring to boil, reduce heat, simmer gently covered 30 minutes, remove lid, simmer further 15 minutes, cool.

Add drained, rinsed beans to cold meat mixture, mix well. Roll out one packet of puff pastry very thinly on lightly floured surface, cut into rounds with 9cm cutter. Put a teaspoon of mixture onto each round, glaze edges of pastry with beaten egg, fold in half, press edges together. Repeat using second packet of pastry. Deep-fry, a few at a time, in hot oil until golden brown. Drain turnovers on absorbent paper.
Makes about 40.

From left: Chicken Wings with Shallots; Smoked Eel and Chive Spread; Mini Flaky Pizzas and Mexican Meat Turnovers.

CAMEMBERT ROLL

Make several days in advance.

150g can camembert
125g cheddar cheese
2 tablespoons mayonnaise
2 teaspoons french mustard
6 shallots
pepper
125g smoked almonds

Remove rind from camembert, put camembert and grated cheddar cheese, mayonnaise, mustard, finely chopped shallots and pepper in small bowl of electric mixer, beat until combined. Form cheese mixture into log shape, roll in finely chopped almonds. Wrap cheese log in aluminium foil, refrigerate until firm.

STUFFED MUSHROOMS

Make stuffing the day before required; fill stuffing into mushrooms several hours before baking

375g mushrooms, approximately 2.5cm in diameter
2 rashers bacon
¼ cup grated cheddar cheese
¼ teaspoon french mustard
1 cup fresh breadcrumbs
1 egg
¼ cup milk
1 tablespoon chopped parsley
salt, pepper
1 tomato
2 slices cheddar cheese, extra

Remove stems from mushrooms. Remove rind from bacon, chop bacon finely. Heat pan, add bacon, cook until golden brown. Remove pan from heat, add grated cheese, mustard and breadcrumbs, mix well. Add lightly beaten egg and milk, parsley, salt and pepper, mix until well combined. Fill stuffing into cavity of mushrooms. Cut extra cheese slices into 1cm squares. Slice tomato, then cut each slice into 8 small segments. Place 1 square of cheese on top of each mushroom; then top with 1 segment of tomato. Place stuffed mushrooms on oven trays; bake in moderately hot oven 8 minutes, or until cheese has melted.

VOL-AU-VENTS WITH SAVORY FILLINGS

Each Filling makes enough for about 24 cases. Fillings can be spooned in several hours ahead; put filled vol-au-vents into moderate oven to heat 15 minutes before serving.

SAUCE

45g butter
2 tablespoons flour
1 cup milk
¼ cup dry white wine
½ x 300ml carton cream
salt, pepper
6 packets 2.5cm vol-au-vent cases (12 cases in each packet)

Heat butter in pan, add flour, stir until well combined, cook 1 minute. Remove from heat, gradually stir in milk, mix until smooth. Return to heat, stir until sauce boils and thickens. Add cream and wine, cook further 1 minute. Season with salt and pepper. Divide sauce into 3 portions. Fill vol-au-vent cases with teaspoonfuls of prepared filling. Bake uncovered in moderate oven about 10 minutes.

OYSTER FILLING

30 oysters
2 teaspoons chopped parsley

Add oysters and parsley to one third of the hot Sauce.

SEAFOOD FILLING

375g green prawns
125g scallops
15g butter
2 shallots
1 teaspoon curry powder

Shell and devein prawns, chop roughly. Clean scallops, chop roughly. Heat butter in pan, add chopped shallots and curry powder; cook 1 minute. Add prawns and scallops, cook 1 minute. Combine seafood with one third of the hot Sauce.

CHICKEN FILLING

1 whole chicken breast
½ x 190g can champignons
2 shallots

Place chicken breast with enough water to cover in pan, bring to boil, reduce heat, simmer covered 15 minutes. Remove chicken from stock. Remove skin and bones, chop meat finely. Combine chicken with drained and finely chopped champignons and chopped shallots. Combine chicken with one third of the hot Sauce.

Stuffed Mushrooms, Camembert Roll and Vol-au-vents with Oyster, Seafood and Chicken Fillings make an atttractive display on a platter.

PANCAKES & CREPES

Wholemeal pancakes are delightfully homely and the other three recipes are rich and delectable; definitely dinner party material.

STRAWBERRY LIQUEUR PANCAKES

PANCAKES
½ cup plain flour
2 eggs
¾ cup milk
FILLING
250g cottage cheese
1 egg yolk
2 tablespoons sugar
1 teaspoon grated orange rind
½ punnet strawberries
SAUCE
30g butter
½ cup sugar
¼ cup orange juice
1½ tablespoons Grand Marnier
½ punnet strawberries
125g frozen or fresh raspberries or boysenberries

Sift flour into bowl, add eggs, stir until mixture is smooth. Gradually stir in milk, mix to a smooth batter; stand 30 minutes. From jug pour 2 to 3 tablespoons of batter into heated, greased pan. Cook until light golden brown. Toss or turn pancake, cook other side. Repeat with remaining batter.

Filling: Combine sieved cottage cheese with egg yolk, sugar and orange rind, mix well. Slice strawberries. Add to cottage cheese mixture, spread mixture evenly over each pancake, roll up, top with hot Sauce. Serve with whipped cream and extra strawberries if desired.

Sauce: Place strawberries and thawed raspberries into food processor or blender, process until pureed. Sieve to remove seeds. Heat butter in pan, add sugar, stir until combined. Add orange juice, Grand Marnier and pureed berries, stir to combine. Bring Sauce to the boil.

Serves 4.

MANGO LIQUEUR PANCAKES

PANCAKES
½ cup plain flour
2 eggs
¾ cup milk
FILLING
125g butter
4 tablespoons sugar
⅔ cup orange juice
2 tablespoons Cointreau or Grand Marnier
2 tablespoons brandy
2 x 470g cans sliced mangos

Sift flour into bowl, add eggs, stir until mixture is smooth. Gradually stir in milk, mix to smooth batter, stand for 30 minutes. Heat pan, grease well. From a small jug pour 2 to 3 tablespoons of pancake mixture into pan, swirling batter evenly around pan. Cook until light golden brown. Toss or turn pancake, cook other side. Repeat with remaining batter.

Filling: Melt butter in pan, add sugar, stir until sugar is golden brown, add orange juice, stir until sugar is dissolved. Add Cointreau and brandy, set aflame. When flames die, simmer sauce gently 2 minutes, remove pan from heat. Drain mango slices, cut into pieces of desired size. Divide mango pieces between pancakes, fold each pancake into half, then into quarters. Place into sauce, return pan to heat, simmer 2 minutes or until pancakes are heated through, spooning sauce over the pancakes. If desired, serve with ice cream or whipped cream.

Serves 4.

WHOLEMEAL PANCAKES WITH LEMON

Stir pancake mixture before each pouring so flour does not settle in jug.
3 eggs
½ cup wholemeal self-raising flour
½ cup wholemeal plain flour
¾ cup water
¾ cup milk
butter
raw sugar
lemon juice

Sift flours into bowl, return husks to bowl. Make well in centre of dry ingredients; add lightly beaten eggs, milk and water; mix to combine. Do not over-beat. Refrigerate 1 hour. Heat pan, grease well. From a small jug pour 2 to 3 tablespoons of pancake mixture into heated, greased pan. Cook until mixture is set and golden brown underneath. Turn pancake and cook on other side. Repeat with remaining batter.

Place pancakes on warm individual plates; rub hot side with plenty of butter until melted. Sprinkle with raw sugar and lemon juice, roll up; serve immediately.

Makes 12 pancakes.

HAZELNUT CREPES WITH ICECREAM AND CHOCOLATE SAUCE

HAZELNUT CREPES
½ cup plain flour
¼ cup ground hazelnuts
3 eggs
2 teaspoons oil
¾ cup milk
HAZELNUT PRALINE ICECREAM
1 litre carton vanilla icecream
½ cup sugar
½ cup roasted hazelnuts
CHOCOLATE SAUCE
15g butter
125g dark cooking chocolate
2 eggs
2 tablespoons sugar
30g glace ginger
1 tablespoon brandy

Combine flour and hazelnuts in bowl, make well in centre. Gradually beat in combined eggs, oil and milk; stand one hour before using. Pour 2 tablespoons of batter into hot, greased pan, toss or turn when brown underneath. Keep warm, serve with Icecream and Chocolate Sauce.

Hazelnut Praline Icecream: Melt sugar in pan over medium heat until golden brown, remove from heat, add nuts. Pour mixture onto greased oven tray; cool. Chop toffee mixture, fold into softened icecream, return icecream to freezer; freeze until firm.

Chocolate Sauce: Combine butter, chocolate, egg, sugar and chopped ginger in top part of double saucepan, stir over simmering water until chocolate has melted, stir in brandy.

Serves 6.

Back: Strawberry Liqueur Pancakes (left); Wholemeal Pancakes with Lemon. Front: Hazelnut Crepes (left); Mango Liqueur Pancakes.

22

Pancakes and crepes are easy to make, so choose one of the recipes, make a batch and store (layered with freezer or plastic food wrap) in the freezer for a month. Then, when required, fill, heat and serve.

SPINACH PANCAKES WITH RICOTTA CHEESE
SPINACH PANCAKES
½ cup plain flour
2 eggs
2 teaspoons oil
1¼ cups milk
250g packet frozen chopped spinach
RICOTTA CHEESE FILLING
2 tablespoons pinenuts
250g ricotta cheese
2 tablespoons grated parmesan cheese
salt, pepper
TOMATO-ONION SAUCE
400g can tomatoes
30g butter
1 clove garlic
1 onion
½ cup water

Sift flour, add eggs and oil; gradually stir in milk. Put spinach in pan, stir occasionally until thawed and liquid evaporated. Stir into batter. Pour ¼ cup batter into greased, heated pan. Repeat with remaining batter. Cook slowly until golden underneath, turn, brown other side. Put a tablespoon of Filling in centre of each pancake, fold in half, then in half again. Place in greased, shallow, ovenproof dish, cover, bake in moderate oven 15 minutes.

Ricotta Cheese Filling: Stir pinenuts over low heat until golden, allow to cool. Beat ricotta cheese with parmesan cheese, pinenuts, salt and pepper.

Tomato-Onion Sauce: Saute crushed garlic and finely chopped onion in butter. Add mashed, undrained tomatoes and water, bring to boil, reduce heat, simmer uncovered 15 minutes. Strain, reheat.

Serves 4.

CREAMY CHICKEN AND VEGETABLE PANCAKES
PANCAKES
1 cup plain flour
2 eggs
1 cup milk, approximately
FILLING
3 chicken breast fillets
1 sprig parsley
1 small onion
½ cup dry white wine
½ cup water
3 black peppercorns
30g butter
1½ tablespoons flour
½ cup cream
1 teaspoon french mustard
salt, pepper
1 stick celery
2 carrots
15g butter, extra
TOPPING
60g cheddar cheese
1 tablespoon grated parmesan cheese
30g roasted hazelnuts

Sift flour into bowl, make well in centre. Add eggs, work flour in from sides; gradually stir in enough milk to make a smooth batter, stand 30 minutes. From small jug pour 2 or 3 tablespoons of batter into heated, greased pan; cook slowly until set and lightly browned underneath. Toss or turn, brown on other side. Repeat with remaining batter.

Filling: Place chicken fillets in pan, add parsley, peppercorns, sliced onion, wine and water. Cover, bake in moderate oven 15 minutes. Remove chicken from pan, cool; strain pan juices, reserve ⅔ cup. Slice chicken finely; cut carrots into thin strips; cut celery into thin strips. Melt butter in pan, stir in flour, then pan juices and cream. Stir until sauce comes to boil, remove from heat. Stir in mustard, salt and pepper. Melt extra butter in pan, add celery and carrot strips, stir over heat until vegetables are just tender. Combine chicken, sauce and vegetables, mix well.

Divide Filling evenly between pancakes, roll up pancakes, place in ovenproof dish, sprinkle combined grated cheddar cheese and parmesan over pancakes. Sprinkle with finely chopped nuts, bake uncovered in moderately hot oven 10 to 15 minutes or until heated through.

Serves 6.

MOUSSAKA CREPES
CREPES
1 cup plain flour
3 eggs
1¼ cups milk
15g butter
FILLING
1 small eggplant
6 shallots
½ teaspoon dried oregano
1 clove garlic
salt, pepper
2 tablespoons oil
250g minced lamb
60g butter
2 ripe tomatoes
2 teaspoons tomato paste
⅓ cup fresh breadcrumbs
2 tablespoons grated parmesan cheese
CHEESE SAUCE
30g butter
1 tablespoon flour
1 cup milk
salt, pepper
¼ cup cream
¼ teaspoon dry mustard
2 tablespoons grated cheddar cheese

Sift flour into bowl, add eggs, melted butter and 2 tablespoons of the milk. Beat until smooth. Beat in remainder of milk; stand 30 minutes. From small jug, pour 2 to 3 tablespoons mixture into heated, greased pan. Cook slowly until set and lightly browned underneath. Turn, brown other side, repeat with remaining batter.

Filling: Chop unpeeled eggplant into small dice, sprinkle with salt and let stand 30 minutes. Rinse under cold running water and drain on kitchen paper. Heat oil in pan, add lamb, cook, stirring for 10 minutes, remove from pan. Melt butter in pan, add eggplant, chopped shallots, oregano and crushed garlic, cook 1 minute. Add peeled and chopped tomatoes and tomato paste, cook 1 minute; remove from pan. Add breadcrumbs, parmesan cheese and half cup of the Cheese Sauce, mix thoroughly. Season with salt and pepper. Place 2 tablespoons of Filling on one end of crepe, roll up, tucking in sides. Repeat with remaining mixture. Arrange crepes in shallow ovenproof dish. Pour over remaining Cheese Sauce, bake, uncovered, in moderate oven 15 minutes.

Cheese Sauce: Melt butter in pan add flour and cook 1 minute. Add milk, stir until mixture boils and thickens; remove from heat. Season with salt and pepper, add cream, mustard and cheese; mix thoroughly.

Serves 6.

From back: Creamy Chicken and Vegetable Pancakes; Moussaka Crepes; Spinach Pancakes with Ricotta Cheese.

QUICHES

Serve an ever-popular hot quiche as a main course with a crisp salad, or serve a small wedge of cold quiche as a summer entree.

SCALLOP AND ZUCCHINI QUICHE
1 cup plain flour
90g butter
1 tablespoon sour cream
FILLING
125g scallops
500g zucchini
1 teaspoon salt
30g butter
1 onion
1 clove garlic
1 teaspoon curry powder
½ cup water
¼ cup dry white wine
30g butter, extra
2 eggs
½ cup cream
2 tablespoons grated parmesan cheese

Sift flour into bowl, rub in butter, mix to a pliable dough with sour cream. Cover, refrigerate 30 minutes. Roll out pastry to line 23cm flan tin. Bake in moderately hot oven 10 minutes or until light golden brown; cool.

When cold, spoon in Filling and sprinkle with parmesan cheese.

Bake in moderate oven 25 minutes or until filling is set.

Filling: Grate zucchini, place in bowl, stir in salt, stand 1 hour. Melt butter, add chopped onion, crushed garlic and curry powder, cook until onion is tender then remove from heat. Place water and wine in pan, bring to boil, reduce heat, add scallops. Cook 1 minute; drain.

Rinse zucchini under cold running water; squeeze out excess water. Melt extra butter in pan, add zucchini, cook 2 minutes. Combine zucchini, scallops, onion mixture, lightly beaten eggs and cream.

QUICK ZUCCHINI QUICHE

If you have frozen breadcrumbs on hand, this is as quick a quiche as you will find.

1 cup wholemeal breadcrumbs
5 small zucchini
1 small onion
1 clove garlic
4 eggs
300ml jar cream
3 tablespoons grated parmesan cheese
1 cup grated cheddar cheese
1 tablespoon self-raising flour
salt, pepper
1 large tomato

Spread crumbs evenly over base of well-greased 25cm flan dish or pie plate (do not use flan tin with removable base). Combine coarsely grated unpeeled zucchini, chopped onion and crushed garlic, add lightly beaten eggs, cream, cheeses and flour, mix well. Season with salt and pepper, spoon gently over crumbs, top with sliced tomato. Bake in moderate oven 45 minutes.

HERBED HAM QUICHE
½ cup white self-raising flour
½ cup wholemeal plain flour
90g butter
1 egg yolk
1 tablespoon lemon juice, approximately
FILLING
200g cottage cheese
150ml can evaporated milk
3 eggs
1 tablespoon french mustard
185g ham
1 tablespoon chopped chives
1 small green pepper
90g cheddar cheese

Sift flours into bowl, return husks from sifter to bowl. Rub in butter, add egg yolk and enough lemon juice to mix to a firm dough. Cover, refrigerate 30 minutes.

Roll pastry to fit 23cm flan tin, cover pastry with greaseproof paper, cover paper thickly with beans or rice. Bake in moderately hot oven 10 minutes, remove paper and beans, bake further 5 minutes. Pour Filling into pastry case, sprinkle with grated cheese. Bake in moderate oven 30 minutes.

Filling: Place cottage cheese, milk, eggs and mustard in food processor or blender, process until smooth. Stir in finely chopped ham, chives and chopped green pepper.

PUMPKIN QUICHE
½ cup wholemeal self-raising flour
½ cup wholemeal plain flour
125g butter
1 egg yolk
2 teaspoons lemon juice, approximately
FILLING
500g pumpkin
2 rashers bacon
3 shallots
1 clove garlic
250g feta cheese
3 eggs
⅔ cup cream
2 tablespoons chopped parsley
pepper

Sift flours into basin, return husks from sifter to basin, rub in butter, add egg yolk and enough lemon juice to just combine ingredients. Cover, refrigerate 30 minutes. Roll pastry to fit 23cm flan tin, bake in moderately hot oven 10 minutes. Pour in Filling, bake in moderate oven further 30 minutes or until set.

Filling: Peel pumpkin, boil or steam in usual way until tender, drain well, cool. Chop bacon finely, cook in pan until crisp, add chopped shallots and crushed garlic, cook few minutes. Push cheese and pumpkin through sieve, add lightly beaten eggs, cream, parsley and pepper, mix well, add bacon mixture.

Clockwise from top left: Scallop and Zucchini Quiche; Herbed Ham Quiche; Pumpkin Quiche; Quick Zucchini Quiche.

LEEK QUICHE

4 sheets packaged filo pastry
45g butter
4 small leeks
45g butter, extra
1 clove garlic
125g feta cheese
⅔ cup cream
3 eggs
pepper

Melt butter, brush each layer of pastry, fold each layer over in half, layer pastry, one folded piece on top of the other to give eight layers. Place pie plate (base measures 18cm) upside down on layered pastry; using plate as a guide, cut around plate making circle 1cm larger than plate. Lift all layers of pastry into plate carefully, leave pastry standing up around edge of plate.

Trim ends from leeks, leave about 5cm of the green tops, slice leeks finely, wash well under cold running water, drain well. Melt extra butter in pan, add leeks and crushed garlic, cook about 5 minutes over low heat until leeks are just tender. Add sieved cheese, cream and lightly beaten eggs, mix well; season with pepper. Pour mixture into pastry case, bake in moderate oven 30 minutes, or until golden brown.

TOMATO AND BASIL QUICHE

1 cup plain flour
90g butter
1 egg yolk
1 tablespoon lemon juice, approximately
FILLING
30g butter
1 leek
3 eggs
300ml carton cream
¾ cup grated cheese
3 small ripe tomatoes
¾ cup chopped fresh basil
½ cup chopped parsley
salt, pepper
1 tablespoon parmesan cheese

Sift flour into bowl, rub in butter, add egg yolk and enough lemon juice to mix to firm dough. Cover, refrigerate 30 minutes. Roll out to fit 23cm flan tin, trim edges. Line tin with greaseproof paper, fill with dry beans or rice, bake in moderately hot oven 10 minutes. Remove paper and beans, return to oven, bake further 5 minutes.
Filling: Melt butter in pan, add sliced leek, cook until tender. Combine eggs, cream and cheese in bowl, add leek, pour into pastry case.

Peel tomatoes, cut into 1cm slices. Roll edge of tomato slices in combined basil and parsley, place on top of leek mixture. Sprinkle with salt, pepper and grated parmesan cheese. Bake in moderate oven 30 minutes.

Left: Leek Quiche; right: Tomato and Basil Quiche.

SOUFFLES

There's no secret to making souffles. The basis is simply a white sauce to which egg yolks and flavorings are added, then egg whites folded in lightly. Savory souffles make a perfect entree or, served with salad, a light main course. Sweet souffles are delicious for dessert.

CHESTNUT SOUFFLE WITH CHOCOLATE CREAM

Sweetened chestnut spread is an imported product available at gourmet food stores and delicatessens. Buy the can which specifies that sugar and vanilla have been added, not the canned chestnut puree.

45g butter
2 tablespoons plain flour
250g can sweetened chestnut
 spread
½ cup milk
4 eggs, separated
2 egg whites, extra
CHOCOLATE CREAM
300ml jar thickened cream
60g dark cooking chocolate
1 tablespoon brandy

Melt butter in pan, add flour, cook 1 minute, stirring constantly. Add milk, stir until sauce boils and thickens. Add chestnut spread and egg yolks, stir over low heat until combined. Beat all egg whites until soft peaks form, fold one third egg whites into chestnut mixture, then pour chestnut mixture into egg whites, gently fold through.

Grease 6 souffle dishes (¾ cup capacity) with butter, coat sides and base with sugar, shake away excess. Divide mixture between dishes. Bake in moderately hot oven 12 to 15 minutes. Sprinkle top with icing sugar if desired. Serve immediately.

Chocolate Cream: Melt chocolate over hot water; cool. Add chocolate to cream, beat until soft peaks form. Fold in brandy, refrigerate.

Serves 6.

APRICOT SOUFFLES
125g dried apricots
⅔ cup dry white wine
2.5cm piece lemon rind
2 teaspoons arrowroot
60g butter
⅓ cup sugar
3 eggs, separated

Place apricots in pan with wine, cook over medium heat uncovered until liquid has evaporated. Puree apricots and lemon rind, add arrowroot, butter cut in small pieces, sugar and egg yolks. Process until completely smooth. Beat egg whites until firm peaks form, gently fold in apricot puree. Pour into six greased individual souffle dishes of ½ cup capacity, or one large dish. Place in baking dish with warm water to come halfway up sides. Lightly butter a piece of aluminium foil and place loosely on top. Bake in moderately hot oven 30 minutes for small souffles; 40 minutes for a large souffle. Serve immediately.

Serves 6.

SPINACH SOUFFLE WITH FRESH TOMATO SAUCE

30g butter
1 onion
250g packet frozen spinach
salt, pepper
¼ teaspoon ground nutmeg
3 tablespoons grated parmesan cheese
60g butter, extra
2½ tablespoons plain flour
¾ cup milk
3 eggs, separated
1 egg white, extra
¼ cup packaged dry breadcrumbs

TOMATO SAUCE
60g butter
1 clove garlic
500g ripe tomatoes
½ teaspoon sugar

Melt butter in pan, add finely chopped onion, cook until onion is tender. Place frozen spinach in separate pan, stir over low heat until spinach is thawed and dried out. Stir spinach into onion, season with salt and pepper, add nutmeg and parmesan cheese; melt extra butter in separate pan, add flour, cook 1 minute, stirring constantly. Add milk, stir until mixture boils and thickens; cool slightly. Add egg yolks one at a time, beating well after each addition. Stir in spinach mixture. Beat egg whites until firm peaks form, lightly fold spinach mixture into egg whites.

Grease six ¾-cup capacity souffle dishes or one large dish, sprinkle with breadcrumbs, shake away excess. Pour souffle mixture into dishes, place on oven tray, bake in moderately hot oven approximately 12 minutes for small souffles; 25 to 30 minutes for a large soufle, or until puffed and golden brown on top. Serve with hot Tomato Sauce.

Tomato Sauce: Melt butter in pan, add crushed garlic and roughly chopped tomatoes. Bring to boil, reduce heat and simmer covered 15 minutes. Push mixture through sieve into pan; discard skin and seeds. Season with sugar, salt and pepper.

Serves 6.

MOUSSES

A mousse can be sweet or savory, hot or cold. We've chosen six superb cold mousses; make them the day before serving if desired.

ONE STEP VELVET CHOCOLATE MOUSSE
300ml jar thickened cream
200g dark cooking chocolate
¼ cup brown sugar, firmly packed
4 egg yolks
1 tablespoon Grand Marnier
1 teaspoon vanilla
2 teaspoons grated orange rind
60g unsalted butter
TOPPING
1 orange
¾ cup water
½ cup sugar
½ cup thickened cream
2 teaspoons Grand Marnier

Heat cream in pan until bubbles form around edges; do not boil. Place chopped chocolate, sugar, egg yolks, Grand Marnier, orange rind and vanilla in blender or processor. Pour in hot cream while blending on high speed for about 1 minute. Drop butter in a teaspoonful at a time, continue to blend until smooth. Pour into 8 small serving glasses, refrigerate 1 to 2 hours before serving. Top with Grand Marnier cream and Orange Strips.

Topping: Peel rind from orange with vegetable peeler. Bring pan of water to boil, add rind, boil 5 minutes; drain. Cut into thin strips. Combine water and sugar in pan, stir over heat until sugar is dissolved, bring to boil, add orange rind and cook until rind is transparent; about 4 minutes. Remove rind from pan, place on aluminium foil until cool. Beat cream and Grand Marnier until thick.

Serves 8.

BERRY CREAM MOUSSE
2 eggs, separated
⅓ cup sugar
¼ cup milk
250g frozen or fresh raspberries
3 teaspoons gelatine
2 tablespoons water
300ml jar thickened cream
1 punnet strawberries

Thaw raspberries to room temperature. Stir egg yolks, sugar and milk in pan over low heat until slightly thickened; do not boil, remove from heat. Puree raspberries in blender or processor, then push through a fine sieve, add to egg yolk mixture. Sprinkle gelatine over cold water, dissolve over hot water, add to raspberry mixture when cool. Beat cream until soft peaks form, fold raspberry mixture into three quarters of the cream. Beat egg whites until soft peaks form, fold gently into mixture. Reserve 6 strawberries for decoration. Slice remaining strawberries finely. Refrigerate raspberry mixture until thick but not set, fold sliced strawberries into mixture. Spoon into six individual dishes, refrigerate until set. Use remaining cream and reserved strawberries to decorate each mousse.

Serves 6.

COCONUT MOUSSE WITH APRICOT SAUCE

Coconut cream can be bought packaged, canned or in a carton. If using the packaged variety, cut off 60g. Use 2 tablespoons of the carton or canned type.

COCONUT MOUSSE
125g white chocolate
60g packaged coconut cream
300ml jar thickened cream
3 teaspoons gelatine
2 tablespoons white rum
2 egg whites
APRICOT SAUCE
125g dried apricots
2½ cups water
2 tablespoons sugar

Melt chopped chocolate over hot water, stir in coconut cream, cool slightly. Beat cream until soft peaks form, fold in chocolate mixture. Sprinkle gelatine over rum, dissolve over hot water, add to coconut cream mixture. Beat egg whites until soft peaks form, gently fold into mixture. Pour into 6 small souffle dishes, refrigerate several hours or until set.

Apricot Sauce: Place chopped apricots and water in pan, cover, simmer 20 minutes or until apricots are soft, add sugar, blend or process until smooth. Depending on apricots, a little more water may need to be added at this stage to make a thin pouring sauce.

Serves 6.

SPINACH AND PISTACHIO MOUSSE
1 bunch spinach (about 8 leaves)
60g butter
1 clove garlic
1 small onion
¼ teaspoon dried basil leaves
3 teaspoons gelatine
2 tablespoons water
60g pistachio nuts
¾ cup thickened cream
1 egg white
salt, pepper

Wash spinach, do not dry, cut away white stalks. Chop leaves roughly, place spinach leaves in pan without extra water. Cover, simmer gently 5 minutes until spinach is soft, cool. Melt butter in pan, add crushed garlic, chopped onion and basil, cook until onion is transparent; cool.

Sprinkle gelatine over water, dissolve over hot water. Place spinach, onion mixture, gelatine mixture, shelled pistachio nuts and cream in processor or blender, process until spinach is finely chopped. Fold in softly beaten egg white. Season with salt and pepper. Pour mixture into individual dishes or mould and refrigerate several hours or overnight.

Serves 6.

JELLIED GAZPACHO
2 tomatoes
1 small green pepper
1 cucumber
1 onion
2 cups tomato juice
1 tablespoon tomato paste
salt, pepper
pinch sugar
1½ tablespoons gelatine
3 tablespoons water

Peel and roughly chop tomatoes; roughly chop pepper, peel and slice half the cucumber; chop onion. Place vegetables in blender or processor, process until finely chopped. Combine vegetables, tomato juice and tomato paste. Season with salt, pepper and sugar.

Sprinkle gelatine over water, dissolve over hot water, stir into tomato mixture. Pour into lightly oiled 20cm ring tin. Refrigerate until set. Turn onto serving dish, decorate with remaining cucumber.

Serves 6 to 8.

Above, from left: Spinach and Pistachio Mousse; Jellied Gazpacho; Egg Mousse. Opposite, from left: Coconut Mousse with Apricot Sauce; One-Step Velvet Chocolate Mousse; Berry Cream Mousse.

EGG MOUSSE
6 hard boiled eggs
¾ cup mayonnaise
3 teaspoons gelatine
¾ cup chicken stock
½ cup thickened cream
1 tablespoon anchovy sauce
3 drops tabasco
1 tomato
4 black olives
watercress

Shell eggs, chop roughly; combine with mayonnaise. Add gelatine to stock, stir over low heat until dissolved, cool slightly. Add gelatine to eggs, mix well. Fold in softly beaten cream, anchovy sauce and tabasco. Pour mixture into lightly oiled 20cm sandwich tin, refrigerate until set, garnish with sliced tomato, halved olives and watercress.

Serves 6.

PIZZAS

Here are 6 fabulous pizza toppings with a choice of 5 different crusts. All topping and base recipes will make 2 pizzas; use pans with base measuring 28cm. If two pizzas are one too many, freeze one (uncooked) for next time. To serve, unwrap frozen pizza, return to pan and bake as directed in individual recipes. Cooking time will be up to 10 minutes longer. If using compressed yeast, use 15g instead of 7g sachet.

QUICK MIX CRISPY CRUST
7g sachet dried yeast
1 teaspoon sugar
¾ cup warm water
2 cups plain flour
pinch salt
Stir water into yeast and sugar, make well in centre of sifted flour and salt, stir in yeast mixture, mix to firm dough, knead on floured surface until smooth. Divide dough in half, roll each half large enough to cover base of two 28cm pizza pans.

WHOLEGRAIN CRISPY CRUST
1½ cups wholemeal plain flour
¼ cup kibble rye
7g sachet dried yeast
1 teaspoon sugar
pinch salt
2 tablespoons oil
½ cup warm water

Combine sifted flour, kibble rye, yeast, sugar and salt in bowl; make well in centre, add oil and warm water, mix to firm dough. Turn on to floured surface, knead 10 to 15 minutes or until dough is smooth and elastic. Place in lightly oiled bowl, cover, stand in warm place 30 minutes or until dough has doubled in bulk. Knock dough down, divide in half, knead each half into a ball. Roll out each to cover base of two 28cm pizza pans.

SCONE CRUST
2 cups self-raising flour
pinch salt
30g butter
1 to 1½ cups milk
oil

Sift flour and salt into basin, rub in butter. Add enough milk to mix to a firm dough. Knead lightly on floured surface until smooth, divide in half, roll each half out to fit two 28cm pizza pans. Brush dough lightly with oil.
Wholemeal variation: Substitute wholemeal self-raising flour for white flour, follow same method.

THICK PIZZA CRUST
1 teaspoon sugar
1⅓ cups water
7g sachet dried yeast
4 cups plain flour
1 teaspoon salt
2 tablespoons oil

Dissolve sugar in warm water, sprinkle yeast over, stand in a warm place 10 minutes. Sift flour and salt into a large bowl, stir in yeast mixture, then oil, knead until smooth on lightly floured surface for 10 to 15 minutes. Place dough in a lightly oiled bowl, cover, stand in warm place 45 minutes or until doubled in bulk. Knock back dough, divide in half, roll each half to fit into two 28cm pizza pans.

RATATOUILLE TOPPING
1 eggplant
salt
¼ cup oil
2 onions
2 cloves garlic
2 red peppers
2 green peppers
3 zucchini
4 tomatoes
¼ cup tomato paste
½ teaspoon each dried thyme, oregano and basil
2 tablespoons grated parmesan cheese
250g mozzarella cheese

Chop eggplant into 1cm pieces, sprinkle well with salt, stand 10 minutes, rinse well in running water, pat dry.

Heat oil in pan, add peeled and chopped onions, cook, stirring over medium heat 10 minutes or until lightly browned; add crushed garlic, chopped peppers (reserve ½ red pepper for top) chopped zucchini, peeled and chopped tomatoes, tomato paste and herbs, cook uncovered over low heat for 30 minutes or until most of the liquid has evaporated. Divide mixture over two pizza bases. Spinkle with parmesan cheese, top with strips of mozzarella cheese and reserved red pepper. Bake in hot oven 20 to 30 minutes.

BACON AND SPINACH TOPPING
6 rashers bacon
1 tablespoon oil
2 cloves garlic
4 onions
1 bunch spinach (about 6 large leaves)
salt, pepper
½ cup sour cream
250g swiss cheese
½ cup grated parmesan cheese

Chop bacon, fry in pan until crisp, remove from pan leaving 1 tablespoon of bacon drippings; add oil, crushed garlic and sliced onions, stir fry in hot oil few minutes or until transparent. Remove from pan, add chopped spinach, stir fry few minutes or until spinach is just beginning to wilt, season with salt and pepper.

Combine sour cream with grated swiss cheese, spread over two pizza bases, top with onions, spinach and bacon. Sprinkle with parmesan cheese, bake in hot oven 20 to 30 minutes.

CHICKEN AND CORN TOPPING
4 chicken thigh fillets
440g can creamed corn
1 onion
½ cup tomato sauce
½ teaspoon basil
½ teaspoon oregano
salt, pepper
4 rashers bacon
185g cabanossi
grated parmesan cheese

Cook chicken fillets in boiling, salted water 7 minutes, drain, chop chicken finely. Combine with corn and finely chopped onion. Combine tomato sauce with basil, oregano, salt and pepper; spread evenly over two pizza bases, top with chicken mixture. Cut bacon into narrow strips lengthways. Arrange in criss-cross pattern over chicken mixture, sprinkle with sliced cabanossi. Bake in hot oven 20 to 30 minutes. Serve sprinkled with parmesan cheese.

HAM AND PINEAPPLE TOPPING
375g mozzarella cheese
2 onions
2 x 450g cans pineapple pieces
2 green peppers
375g ham

Grate cheese over two pizza bases, top with thinly sliced onions, well drained pineapple, chopped peppers and finely chopped ham. Bake in hot oven 20 to 30 minutes.

THREE CHEESE TOPPING
125g ricotta cheese
125g feta cheese
⅓ cup grated parmesan cheese
30g butter
5 shallots
2 cloves garlic
pepper
60g black olives
2 tomatoes
45g can anchovy fillets

Beat combined cheeses in electric mixer or food processor until smooth. Melt butter in pan, add chopped shallots and crushed garlic, cook, stirring for one minute, cool slightly, stir in cheese mixture, season with pepper. Divide mixture over two pizza bases, top with stoned olives, sliced tomatoes and well-drained anchovy fillets, bake in hot oven 20 to 30 minutes.

PIZZA WITH THE LOT
2 teaspoons oil
1 clove garlic
1 onion
400g can tomatoes
½ teaspoon basil
½ teaspoon oregano
salt, pepper
185g mozzarella cheese
¼ cup grated parmesan cheese
250g salami
1 green pepper
125g mushrooms
45g can anchovy fillets
45g stuffed olives

Heat oil in pan, add crushed garlic and finely chopped onion; cook until onion is transparent. Add undrained tomatoes, mash well. Add basil and oregano, bring to boil, reduce heat, simmer uncovered 15 minutes, stirring occasionally. Season with salt and pepper, cool. Spread over two pizza bases. Combine grated mozzarella cheese with parmesan cheese, sprinkle quarter of mixture over each pizza. Top with sliced salami, finely chopped pepper, sliced mushrooms and well drained and chopped anchovy fillets. Sprinkle with sliced olives and remaining cheese. Bake in hot oven 20 to 30 minutes.

Clockwise, from top: Pizza with The Lot; Ratatouille Topping; Bacon and Spinach Topping; Chicken and Corn Topping; Three Cheese Topping; Ham and Pineapple Topping.

Sauces for Pasta

Pasta is widely available packaged, frozen, or fresh from specialty shops. It comes in many shapes, sizes, colors and flavors, so choose whichever you like to complement our sauces. Cooking time varies: freshly made takes the shortest time. Boil pasta uncovered in a large pan of rapidly boiling, salted water with a couple of teaspoons of oil added to the water. Pasta should be cooked until it is just tender; drain immediately, do not rinse under water.

SEAFOOD PASTA
375g pasta
125g squid
250g scallops
6 oysters
250g cooked prawns
1 cup water
½ cup dry white wine
4 spinach leaves
2 shallots
LEMON-WINE SAUCE
60g butter
1½ cups dry white wine
1 tablespoon lemon juice
½ cup cream
2 teaspoons cornflour
1 tablespoon water
salt, pepper
1 tablespoon chopped chives

Clean squid and cut into 1cm rings. Cut scallops in half. Shell and devein prawns, cut prawns in half lengthwise. Boil water and wine in pan, add squid and scallops, remove from heat, stand 1 minute; drain, reserve liquid for Sauce. Shred spinach finely and chop shallots. Cook pasta in boiling salted water 10 to 15 minutes; drain. Add all seafood, spinach and shallots to pasta and mix well. Pour Sauce over, stir through lightly.

Lemon-Wine Sauce: Melt butter in pan, add wine and boil rapidly until reduced to ¼ cup. Add 1 cup reserved scallop liquid and boil until reduced to ¾ cup. Add lemon juice and cream. Blend cornflour with water, add to sauce, stir until sauce boils and thickens. Season with salt and pepper, add chives before serving.

Serves 6.

CABANOSSI CARBONARA
375g pasta
500g cabanossi sausage
30g butter
¼ cup cream
¼ teaspoon paprika
2 eggs
⅓ cup grated parmesan cheese
½ cup chopped parsley
salt, pepper

Cook pasta in boiling salted water for 10 to 15 minutes; drain.

While pasta is cooking, cook sliced cabanossi in half the butter for few minutes, add cream and paprika, remove from heat. Combine beaten eggs, parmesan cheese and parsley in bowl. While pasta is hot, quickly add the remaining butter, cabanossi and cream mixture, then egg mixture, stir lightly until combined. Season with salt and pepper, serve immediately.

Serves 4.

PASTA WITH AVOCADO

Make this when avocados are cheap and plentiful; it's deliciously creamy.

375g pasta
2 tablespoons olive oil
2 cloves garlic
2 large avocados
1 tablespoon lemon juice
salt, pepper
½ cup grated parmesan cheese
2 tablespoons cream

Cook pasta in boiling salted water for 10 to 15 minutes, drain.

While pasta is cooking, peel and stone avocados, mash with potato masher, do not puree. Mix in lemon juice, season with salt and pepper. Heat oil in pan, add crushed garlic then avocado mixture, heat without boiling; stir in cream.

Pour over hot pasta. Serve with parmesan cheese.

Serves 4.

Above: Cabanossi Carbonara. Opposite: Seafood Pasta (top); Pasta with Avocado.

PASTA WITH CREAMY EGG AND SEAFOOD SAUCE

This is a great way to dress up that can of smoked oysters or mussels into a stunning sauce for pasta.

375g pasta
2 hard-boiled eggs
2½ cups milk
1 clove garlic
60g butter
3 tablespoons plain flour
½ teaspoon dry mustard
salt, pepper
105g can smoked mussels or oysters
3 tablespoons chopped chives
¼ cup grated parmesan cheese

Cook pasta in boiling salted water for 10 to 15 minutes; drain. Blend or process eggs and milk until smooth. Cook crushed garlic in butter for 2 minutes, stir in flour, add egg mixture, mustard, salt and pepper, cook, stirring constantly until mixture boils and thickens, reduce heat, simmer few minutes. Stir in drained oysters or mussels and chives. Serve over hot pasta, sprinkled with parmesan cheese.

Serves 4.

FAMILY STYLE PASTA SAUCE
500g pasta
500g mince
2 tablespoons oil
2 onions
2 cloves garlic
2 carrots
1 stick celery
1 green pepper
1 red pepper
2 x 400g cans tomatoes
¼ cup tomato paste
½ cup dry white wine
1 beef stock cube
1 cup water

Heat oil in pan, cook chopped onion until golden brown. Add crushed garlic, cook one minute, remove from pan, add mince, cook over high heat in batches until well browned; add sliced carrots and celery and chopped peppers, cook covered 10 minutes or until vegetables are just tender. Add undrained crushed tomatoes, return onion to pan; add tomato paste, wine, crumbled stock cube and water. Bring to boil, reduce heat, simmer covered 30 minutes. Cook pasta in boiling salted water 10 to 15 minutes; drain, serve tossed with meat mixture.

Serves 6.

PASTA WITH BASIL AND ALMONDS
45g slivered almonds
185g pasta
1 cup fresh basil leaves
125g butter
1 clove garlic
2 tablespoons cream
salt, pepper

Put almonds on baking tray, bake in moderate oven 5 minutes or until golden brown, cool. Bring large pan of salted water to boil, add pasta, cook 10 minutes, drain. Return pasta to pan, lightly stir in chopped basil, crushed garlic, butter, cream, salt and pepper. Sprinkle with almonds.

Serves 2.

SALADS

The Rainbow Coleslaw and Layered Garden Salad are ideal for barbecues; Greek Fish Salad and Water Chestnut Salad can be served instead of a green salad. A potato salad is always popular; the two prawn salads make perfect main courses.

RAINBOW COLESLAW

Prepare the day before required, add dressing just before serving.

¼ green cabbage
¼ red cabbage
1 onion
2 sticks celery
450g can crushed pineapple
MUSTARD DRESSING
¾ cup mayonnaise
⅓ cup french dressing
1½ teaspoons french mustard
3 tablespoons chopped parsley
salt, pepper

Wash cabbage, shred finely, grate onion. Combine cabbage, onion, chopped celery and drained pineapple. Refrigerate, covered; mix dressing through the salad before serving.
Mustard Dressing: Combine all ingredients; mix well.
   Serves 4 to 6.

LAYERED GARDEN SALAD

Make this colorful salad the day before it is required for the best results.

½ lettuce
250g (2 cups) frozen peas
2 hard boiled eggs
250g mushrooms
125g tasty cheese
1 cup mayonnaise
2 tablespoons sour cream
2 teaspoons french mustard
1 tablespoon lemon juice
6 shallots
1 tomato
4 rashers bacon
2 tablespoons chopped parsley

Shred lettuce coarsely, place in salad bowl. Sprinkle uncooked frozen peas over lettuce, push eggs through sieve, combine with finely sliced mushrooms spread over peas, top with grated cheese. Combine mayonnaise, sour cream, mustard, lemon juice and shallots, pour over cheese. Cover, refrigerate several hours or overnight. Chop bacon finely, fry in pan until crisp; drain. Top with tomato wedges, bacon and parsley just before serving.
Serves 6 to 8.

WATER CHESTNUT SALAD WITH GINGER

230g can water chestnuts
1 small lettuce
1 small bunch watercress
¾ cup alfalfa sprouts
GINGER DRESSING
¼ cup oil
1½ tablespoons dry sherry
1½ tablespoons lemon juice
1 shallot
1 teaspoon grated green ginger
salt, pepper

Drain water chestnuts, rinse under cold water, slice in half. Wash watercress, break into sprigs. Wash lettuce, tear into large pieces. Place water chestnuts, watercress, lettuce and alfalfa sprouts in large bowl, add Ginger Dressing, toss well.
Ginger Sauce Dressing: Combine oil, dry sherry, lemon juice, finely chopped shallot, ginger, salt and pepper in a bowl, mix well.
   Serves 6.

GREEK FISH SALAD

Serve as a main course salad for two, or an entree for four.

4 fish fillets
1 onion
1 green pepper
1 lemon
2 tablespoons chopped parsley
⅓ cup olive oil
salt, pepper

Remove skin from fish; poach or steam fish until tender, cool. Place fish in dish, top with peeled and thinly sliced onion and thinly sliced pepper. Thinly slice half the lemon, add to dish with juice from remaining lemon half. Sprinkle with parsley, add oil, season with salt and pepper; cover, refrigerate several hours or overnight.
Serves 2 to 4.

From back: Layered Garden Salad; Rainbow Coleslaw Salad; Water Chestnut Salad; Greek Fish Salad.

SEAFOOD SALAD WITH CRISPY NOODLES

2 cups water
85g packet chicken flavor
    two-minute noodles
oil for deep frying
250g prawns
1 cup water, extra
salt
1 cucumber
3 spinach leaves
185g scallops
2 sticks celery
125g mushrooms

DRESSING
¼ cup dry white wine
1 tablespoon chopped chives
1 clove garlic
2 tablespoons oil
salt, pepper

Bring water to boil, add contents of one flavor-mix sachet, stir until dissolved. Add noodles, bring to boil. While loosening noodles, reduce heat, simmer uncovered two minutes, drain immediately. Rinse noodles under cold running water then drain well. Spread noodles out on clean tea towel placed over wire rack. Allow to dry three to four hours or overnight in refrigerator.

Divide noodles into about five batches. Heat oil in pan, add one batch, fry until golden brown, turning frequently. Drain on absorbent paper. Repeat with remaining batches.

Shell prawns, reserve shells. Put reserved shells, extra water and salt in pan, bring to boil, reduce heat, simmer uncovered 10 minutes, drain, reserve stock. Score cucumber with fork, cut into thin slices, add reserved stock, reserving ¼ cup for Dressing; stand cucumber 30 minutes, drain.

Wash spinach, remove white stalks, cut leaves roughly. Clean scallops. Cook scallops in boiling water two minutes; drain. Slice celery diagonally, slice mushrooms. Combine spinach, scallops, celery, mushrooms, prawns and drained cucumber, mix well. Line sides of serving dish with noodles, spoon salad in centre, pour dressing over salad.

Dressing: Combine reserved stock, white wine, chives, crushed garlic, oil, salt, pepper.

Serves 6.

From left: Seafood Salad with Crispy Noodles; Hot Potato Salad; Curried Seafood and Rice.

CURRIED SEAFOOD AND RICE

Cook rice the day before required for best results.

1½ cups long grain rice
pinch saffron
250g cooked prawns
125g scallops
3 shallots
1 red pepper
1 green pepper
1 tablespoon chopped chives
salt, pepper

CURRY DRESSING
¼ cup bottled french dressing
½ teaspoon curry powder
¼ teaspoon cumin
pinch cardamom
pinch coriander
salt, pepper

Cook rice with saffron in large pan of boiling salted water 12 minutes. Drain and cool. Shell and devein prawns, chop in large pieces. Cover scallops with boiling water, stand 2 minutes then drain and pat dry. Cut scallops in half. Finely chop shallots; chop peppers. Combine all ingredients in large bowl, add Curry Dressing and toss well. Season with salt and pepper.

Curry Dressing: Combine all ingredients in screw-top jar, shake well until all ingredients are combined.

Serves 6.

HOT POTATO SALAD

2 x 440g cans new potatoes
4 tablespoons chopped parsley
2 tablespoons chopped mint
1 tablespoon chopped chives
2 teaspoons canned green
  peppercorns
⅓ cup mayonnaise
2 tablespoons french dressing
½ cup cream

Drain and rinse potatoes, leave whole or slice thickly. Combine remaining ingredients in pan, add potatoes, heat gently for 5 minutes.

Serves 4 to 6.

FRENCH DRESSING

A combination of oil and vinegar or lemon juice, seasoned with salt and pepper.

The correct proportion for french dressing is three parts oil to one part vinegar or lemon juice, but many people find this gives too oily a dressing and prefer to use less oil.

MAYONNAISE

An emulsion of egg yolk, oil, vinegar and lemon juice.

2 egg yolks
½ teaspoon salt
½ teaspoon dry mustard
1½ teaspoons vinegar
1 cup oil
½ teaspoon lemon juice

Rinse bowl with hot water; dry well. Put in egg yolks, salt, mustard and 1 teaspoon vinegar. Beat vigorously with whisk or at low speed on electric mixer or in food processor; add oil, drop by drop, whisking continuously until a little more than ¼ cup of oil has been added. Add ½ teaspoon vinegar, then very slowly pour in remaining oil in a thin stream, whisking continually. Then add the lemon juice to whiten and flavor.

Makes about 1 cup.

Note: If the oil is added too quickly, it will separate from the egg yolks. If this occurs, place another egg yolk in a clean dry bowl, slowly add the curdled mixture, drop by drop, whisking continuously until all the mixture has been added, then continue with the recipe.

MAIN COURSES

Many varieties of fish are available: choose the best of your local white, non-oily fish for the recipes which specify fillets.

CRUNCHY TOPPED SALMON AND ASPARAGUS
1 cup long grain rice
30g butter
1 tablespoon lemon juice
1 tablespoon chopped parsley
440g can asparagus cuts
TOPPING
60g butter
1 onion
½ cucumber
½ green pepper
2 tablespoons flour
¼ cup water
¼ cup sour cream
220g can salmon
2 teaspoons chopped mint
salt, pepper
60g cheddar cheese
CROUTONS
4 thin slices white bread
oil for deep-frying
2 tablespoons chopped parsley

Cook rice in large pan of boiling salted water 12 minutes; drain well; mix in butter, lemon juice and parsley. Spread over base of ovenproof dish. Drain asparagus, reserve ½ cup liquid; sprinkle asparagus evenly over rice.

Topping: Heat butter in pan, add chopped onion, saute until just tender. Peel and seed cucumber, chop finely, add to onion with chopped pepper, saute 1 minute. Stir in flour, cook 1 minute. Stir in reserved asparagus liquid and water, stir until sauce boils and thickens. Stir in sour cream, drained flaked salmon, mint, salt and pepper. Spoon over asparagus, sprinkle with grated cheese. Bake uncovered in moderate oven 30 minutes, top with Croutons.

Croutons: Remove crusts from bread. Cut bread into small cubes. Deep-fry in hot oil, drain, toss in parsley.

Serves 4.

CURRIED TUNA SLICE
1 cup plain flour
90g butter
1 egg yolk
1 tablespoon water, approximately
FILLING
425g can tuna
2 sticks celery
1 onion
60g butter
2 tablespoons flour
½ cup milk
½ cup water
salt, pepper
2 eggs
3 teaspoons curry powder
45g cheddar cheese
½ teaspoon paprika

Sift flour into bowl, rub in butter, add egg yolk and enough water to mix to a stiff dough, refrigerate 30 minutes. Roll pastry out to fit base of lamington tin (base measures 16cm × 26cm).

Filling: Spread well-drained tuna over pastry. Saute chopped onion and chopped celery in 15g of the butter until onion is transparent, spread over tuna. Melt remaining butter, add flour and 2 teaspoons curry powder, stir until smooth. Add milk and water gradually, stir until sauce boils and thickens, reduce heat, add 30g of the grated cheese, stir until melted, add salt and pepper. Add lightly beaten eggs, mix well.

Spread the cheese sauce evenly over the onion and celery. Combine remaining grated cheese, remaining curry powder and paprika, sprinkle on top of slice. Bake in moderately hot oven for 10 minutes, reduce heat to moderate, bake further 25 to 30 minutes or until light golden brown.

Serves 4 to 6.

SALMON KEDGEREE
220g can red salmon
2 hard-boiled eggs
1 cup long grain rice
90g butter
pepper
⅓ cup chopped parsley
2 teaspoons lemon juice

Cook rice in large quantity of boiling water until tender, about 12 minutes; drain. Drain and flake salmon, shell and chop eggs. Melt butter in pan, add salmon and rice, season with pepper. Stir in chopped eggs, heat through. Lightly stir in parsley and lemon juice.

Serves 2.

Smoked Fish Kedgeree: Substitute 500g smoked fish, poach in water 5 minutes; drain and flake.

Clockwise from left: Smoked Fish with Vegetables; Crunchy Topped Salmon and Asparagus; Salmon Kedgeree; Curried Tuna Slice; Prawns with Feta Cheese.

PRAWNS WITH FETA CHEESE

500g green king prawns
2 tablespoons lemon juice
6 shallots
1 tablespoon chopped parsley
2 cloves garlic
¼ cup oil
400g can tomatoes
2 teaspoons tomato paste
60g butter
¼ cup dry white wine
185g feta cheese

Shell and clean prawns, sprinkle with lemon juice. Heat oil in large pan, stir in chopped shallots, parsley and crushed garlic. Cook 30 seconds, then stir in mashed, undrained tomatoes and tomato paste. Bring sauce to boil, reduce heat, simmer gently uncovered 15 minutes or until sauce is fairly thick. Heat butter in pan, stir in prawns, cook over medium heat until prawns turn pink. Add prawns to the tomato sauce, add wine, mix well. Crumble cheese over prawns and sauce.

Serves 4.

SMOKED FISH WITH VEGETABLES

500g smoked fish
pepper
30g butter
1 red pepper
250g zucchini
2 large tomatoes
1 clove garlic
30g cheddar cheese
2 tablespoons cream

Soak fish in warm water 15 minutes; drain. Cut into large pieces, remove any bones. Bring a pan of water to boil, add fish, return to boil, drain immediately, place in shallow oven-proof dish, season with pepper.

Melt butter in pan, add chopped pepper, fry until soft. Peel and slice tomatoes, add to pan with crushed garlic, cook 5 minutes. Grate zucchini, add to pan, cook further 1 minute.

Pour cream over fish, top with vegetables and grated cheese. Bake uncovered in moderate oven 10 to 15 minutes or until golden brown.

Serves 4.

FISH FILLETS WITH ASPARAGUS

4 fish fillets
salt, pepper
2 slices ham
2 slices swiss cheese
340g can asparagus spears
15g butter
1 tablespoon lemon juice
1 teaspoon cornflour
¼ cup water
2 shallots

Remove skin and bones from fish, sprinkle with salt and pepper. Cut each slice of ham and cheese in half, drain asparagus, cut spears in half. Place 1 slice of ham to one end of fish fillet; top with asparagus and cheese. Fold other end of fillet over; place in lightly greased ovenproof dish. Dot with butter. Repeat with the remaining fish, ham, asparagus and cheese. Cover, bake in moderately hot oven 20 minutes or until tender. Place fish on serving dish, keep warm. Strain juices into pan, add lemon juice and blended cornflour and water, stir over heat until sauce boils and thickens, add chopped shallots; spoon over fish.

Serves 4.

CAMEMBERT AND BACON TOPPED FISH

4 fish fillets
1 tablespoon lemon juice
salt, pepper
2 tablespoons flour
45g butter
4 rashers bacon
2 green peppers
185g can camembert cheese
¼ cup brandy
2 tablespoons flaked almonds
¼ cup grated parmesan cheese
30g butter, extra

Skin and bone fish. Sprinkle with lemon juice, toss in flour seasoned with salt and pepper. Melt butter in pan, cook fish 2 minutes on each side. Place fish in single layer in baking dish. Chop bacon finely, fry until crisp, drain, sprinkle over fish. Cut peppers into rings, place over bacon, top with cubed camembert and brandy. Sprinkle with almonds and parmesan cheese, dot with extra butter. Bake uncovered in moderately hot oven 15 to 20 minutes.

Serves 4.

SEAFOOD AND SPINACH MORNAY

500g fish fillets
125g small cooked prawns
125g scallops
45g butter
3 tablespoons flour
¾ cup milk
¼ cup dry white wine
½ cup cream
60g cheddar cheese
salt, pepper
4 shallots
60g butter, extra

SPINACH RICE

1 cup long grain rice
5 spinach leaves
1 onion
1 clove garlic
30g butter
CRUMB TOPPING
30g butter
1½ cups fresh white breadcrumbs
2 tablespoons chopped parsley

Melt butter in pan, add flour, cook stirring for 1 minute. Gradually add milk and wine, stir until sauce boils and thickens. Add cream and grated cheese, stir over heat until cheese melts; season with salt and pepper.

Shell prawns and clean scallops, remove skin and bones from fish. Cut fish into cubes, finely chop shallots. Melt extra butter in pan, add fish, scallops and shallots, cook 2 minutes, add prawns and sauce, mix well.

Spread Spinach Rice into shallow ovenproof dish, pour seafood mixture over rice, sprinkle with Crumb Topping, bake uncovered in moderate oven 20 minutes or until golden brown.

Spinach Rice: Cook rice in large pan of boiling salted water 12 minutes, drain, cool. Remove stalks from spinach; roughly shred spinach. Place spinach in pan with about ¼ cup hot water, cook covered 3 minutes. Drain well, squeeze out excess water with hand. Heat butter in pan, saute finely chopped onion and crushed garlic, stir in spinach and rice.

Crumb Topping: Melt butter in pan, stir in breadcrumbs and parsley.

Serves 6.

TROUT WITH LEMON PARSLEY BUTTER

There is no need to scale fish cooked this way; the skin will peel away easily with the aluminium foil.

2 trout
60g butter
1 teaspoon grated lemon rind
1 small clove garlic
1 tablespoon chopped parsley
1 tablespoon lemon juice
salt, pepper

Wash and dry trout. Fold a piece of aluminium foil in half for extra strength; foil must be large enough to enclose fish completely. Place fish on foil, wrap tightly, bake on tray in moderately hot oven for 20 minutes. (Fish can be barbecued in this way, too.) Blend softened butter with lemon rind, crushed garlic, parsley and lemon juice, season with salt and pepper, mix well. Serve topped with the butter.

Serves 2.

Clockwise from top left: Seafood and Spinach Mornay; Trout with Lemon Parsley Butter; Fish Fillets with Asparagus; Camembert and Bacon Topped Fish.

Ever-popular chicken makes a low cost meal or, dressed up, something special for an elegant dinner party.

CHICKEN WITH ONION SAUCE
1kg chicken drumsticks
2 tablespoons oil
60g butter
1 onion
400g can tomatoes
41g packet french onion soup mix
1 tablespoon soy sauce
1 cup water
3 teaspoons cornflour
1 tablespoon water, extra

Heat oil and half the butter in pan, add drumsticks and brown; remove from pan. Drain fat from pan, add remaining butter and sliced onion, cook until tender. Add the undrained mashed tomatoes, soup mix, soy sauce and water, heat through. Place chicken in ovenproof dish, pour sauce over, cover, bake in moderate oven 45 minutes. Remove chicken, pour sauce into pan, stir in blended cornflour and extra water, stir until sauce boils and thickens, pour over chicken.
Serves 4.

CHICKEN WINGS RISOTTO
1kg chicken wings
30g butter
2 tablespoons oil
30g butter, extra
1 onion
1 clove garlic
1 red pepper
2 zucchini
4 shallots
1 stick celery
pinch saffron
½ cup dry white wine
1 cup long grain rice
1½ cups water
1 chicken stock cube
2 tablespoons chopped parsley

Trim wing tips at first joint; discard. Heat butter and oil in pan, add wings, cook until golden brown on both sides; drain. Melt extra butter in large pan, add chopped onion and crushed garlic, cook until tender. Add chopped pepper, finely chopped shallots, sliced zucchini, sliced celery and saffron, cook further 1 minute. Add wine, rice, water, crumbled stock cube and chicken wings, bring to boil, cover, reduce heat and simmer for 20 to 25 minutes or until all the liquid is absorbed. Remove from heat, stir in parsley.
Serves 4.

From left: Chicken Wings Risotto; Chicken with Onion Sauce; Chicken with Mushrooms; Crusty Chicken Casserole; Chicken Livers with Vegetables.

CHICKEN WITH MUSHROOMS

4 chicken breast fillets
2 teaspoons oyster sauce
2 teaspoons soy sauce
2 teaspoons cornflour
½ teaspoon sugar
½ teaspoon sesame oil
3 shallots
salt
3 tablespoons oil
1 onion
125g small mushrooms

Cut chicken into 1cm strips, combine with the oyster sauce, soy sauce, cornflour, sugar and sesame oil, mix well, stand 20 minutes. Cut onion into thin wedges, cut shallots into 2.5cm lengths. Heat 1 tablespoon of the oil in pan, add onion, cook until transparent. Add mushrooms and salt, toss over high heat 1 minute, remove from pan. Add remaining 2 tablespoons oil to pan. When oil is hot, add chicken, cook over high heat until golden brown, stirring occasionally. Stir in mushroom mixture and shallots.

Serves 4.

CRUSTY CHICKEN CASSEROLE

1 barbecued or steamed chicken
1 onion
2 shallots
1 stick celery
¼ cup water
30g butter
3 rashers bacon
60g mushrooms
440g can cream of chicken soup
300g carton sour cream
¼ cup grated cheese
CHEESE BATTER
1 cup self-raising flour
½ red pepper
½ green pepper
2 eggs
1 cup grated cheese
½ cup milk

Remove chicken meat from bones, chop meat roughly. Place chopped onion, chopped shallots, chopped celery and water in pan, bring to boil, reduce heat, simmer covered 15 minutes. Melt butter in pan, add chopped bacon and sliced mushrooms, cook 3 minutes. Combine the soup, sour cream, chicken, vegetables and bacon mixture. Pour into greased ovenproof dish. Spread Cheese Batter over top, bake uncovered in moderate oven 40 minutes. Sprinkle with cheese, return to oven for 5 minutes.

Cheese Batter: Sift flour into bowl, add diced peppers, lightly beaten eggs, cheese and milk; mix until just blended.

Serves 4 to 6.

Clockwise from top: Saucy Chicken and Bacon Casserole; Sour Cream and Lemon Chicken; Lemon Chicken with Basil Sauce; Creamy Tarragon Chicken; Chicken with Honey Glaze.

CHICKEN LIVERS WITH VEGETABLES

250g chicken livers
3 chicken thigh fillets
3 teaspoons soy sauce
¼ teaspoon sugar
375g zucchini
3 sticks celery
2 tomatoes
1 tablespoon tomato sauce
oil for frying

Soak livers in cold, salted water 15 minutes, rinse well and drain. Cut each liver into three. Slice chicken fillets thinly, combine with soy sauce and sugar. Cut zucchini into 1cm pieces; slice celery, peel tomatoes, cut into small pieces.

Heat 2 tablespoons oil in pan, add zucchini and celery, cook 2 minutes. Remove vegetables from pan. Add 2 tablespoons oil to pan; when oil is hot add chicken, cook 2 minutes over high heat, stirring occasionally. Add the chicken livers, cook 2 minutes. Add tomatoes, tomato sauce, zucchini and celery; heat through.

Serves 4.

CHICKEN WITH HONEY GLAZE

1 barbecued chicken
½ cup honey
½ cup dry white wine
2 tablespoons chopped chives
1 tablespoon soy sauce
1 tablespoon lemon juice
1 clove garlic
1 teaspoon grated green ginger
1 teaspoon cornflour

Cut chicken into pieces or leave whole, place in ovenproof dish. Combine honey and wine in pan, stir over heat until honey becomes liquid. Blend lemon juice, soy sauce and cornflour together. Add chives, crushed garlic, ginger and cornflour mixture to honey and wine. Stir over heat until sauce boils and thickens slightly. Pour over chicken, bake uncovered in a moderate oven 30 minutes.

Serves 4.

LEMON CHICKEN WITH BASIL SAUCE

This recipe can be prepared up to a day ahead and cooked just before serving. The sauce is best made once the chicken is in the oven.

4 chicken breast fillets
2 rashers bacon
1 cup fresh breadcrumbs
1 teaspoon grated lemon rind
2 teaspoons lemon juice
1 clove garlic
60g butter
½ cup plain flour
30g butter, extra
BASIL SAUCE
2 egg yolks
30g butter
½ cup chicken stock
½ cup cream
¼ cup fresh basil leaves

Chop bacon finely, cook in pan, stirring until crisp. Drain on absorbent paper. Pound chicken fillets thinly. Combine bacon, breadcrumbs, lemon rind, lemon juice, crushed garlic and soft butter. Place in centre of each fillet, fold over, pound edges together lightly, toss in flour. Heat extra butter in pan, add chicken, brown quickly on both sides. Place in ovenproof dish, bake covered in moderately hot oven 10 minutes. Turn fillets, cover, bake further 10 minutes.

Basil Sauce: Put egg yolks in blender, blend while gradually adding melted butter. Pour in chicken stock, cream and basil, blend until smooth. Heat without boiling.

Serves 4.

SOUR CREAM AND LEMON CHICKEN

8 chicken thigh fillets
½ cup sour cream
1 teaspoon grated lemon rind
2 teaspoons lemon juice
1 teaspoon worcestershire sauce
1 tablespoon chopped chives
1 tablespoon chopped parsley
2 cups packaged dry breadcrumbs
1 teaspoon grated lemon rind, extra
2 tablespoons oil
60g butter

Combine the sour cream, lemon rind, worcestershire sauce, lemon juice, chives and parsley. Mix chicken with sour cream mixture, stand 2 to 3 hours or refrigerate overnight. Combine breadcrumbs with extra grated lemon rind. Dip each coated chicken piece in crumbs. Heat oil and butter in pan, fry chicken in single layer until golden brown and tender.

Serves 4.

CREAMY TARRAGON CHICKEN

1 barbecued or steamed chicken
3 shallots
250g mushrooms
30g butter
1 teaspoon dried tarragon leaves
¾ cup cream

Cut chicken into serving sized pieces. Chop shallots, slice mushrooms. Melt butter in pan, add shallots, cook 30 seconds, add tarragon and chicken pieces, cook over low heat 2 minutes. Stir in mushrooms and cream. Cook gently until heated through.

Serves 4.

SAUCY CHICKEN AND BACON CASSEROLE

6 chicken fillets
2 teaspoons oregano
¾ cup plain flour
60g butter
2 tablespoons oil
60g butter, extra
1 clove garlic
4 rashers bacon
4 leeks
6 shallots
250g mushrooms
400g can tomatoes
440g can cream of chicken soup
½ cup dry white wine
3 tablespoons brandy
½ teaspoon chilli sauce
1 teaspoon worcestershire sauce
1 teaspoon soy sauce
½ cup cream
¼ cup chopped chives

Cut chicken fillets into three pieces, toss in combined oregano and flour. Heat butter and oil in pan, add chicken in batches, cook until light golden brown, remove from pan, place in ovenproof dish. Heat extra butter in pan, add crushed garlic, chopped bacon, sliced leeks, chopped shallots and sliced mushrooms, cook few minutes or until mushrooms are soft, add to chicken with undrained mashed tomatoes, undiluted soup, wine, brandy, chilli sauce, worcestershire sauce and soy sauce; mix well. Cover, cook in moderate oven 40 minutes or until chicken is tender. Just before serving, stir in cream and chives.

Serves 6.

Succulent lamb is always popular as family fare or as part of a special dinner menu; be sure not to over-cook lamb. The trend today is to serve lamb slightly under-cooked, but this may not appeal to all tastes.

RATATOUILLE LAMB
1 small shoulder of lamb
45g can anchovy fillets
2 cloves garlic
1 eggplant
1 red pepper
250g zucchini
1 onion
2 tablespoons oil
1 clove garlic, extra
400g can tomatoes

Ask butcher to bone the shoulder. Drain anchovy fillets, reserving oil. Cut anchovies into 1cm pieces. Score skin of lamb about 5cm apart; insert a piece of sliced garlic and a piece of anchovy alternately into flesh; reserve remaining anchovies. Tie meat securely with string at 1cm intervals. Rub skin well with reserved oil. Place in baking dish, cook in hot oven 10 minutes; then reduce heat to moderate, bake further 30 minutes.

Cut eggplant into chunks; cut red pepper into 2.5cm pieces. Slice zucchini thickly, chop onion. Heat oil in pan, add extra crushed garlic, reserved anchovies and onion, cook 1 minute. Add eggplant, cook until onion is transparent, stirring occasionally. Add undrained mashed tomatoes. Bring to boil, add zucchini and red pepper, pour over lamb. Bake uncovered further 10 minutes. Serve lamb sliced with the vegetables.
Serves 4.

RACK OF LAMB WITH MINT BEARNAISE

The cooking time given will result in lamb being slightly pink; increase time by 5 minutes if desired.

4 racks of lamb, with 3 chops
**   in each**
2 tablespoons french mustard
1 tablespoon oil
MINT BEARNAISE
⅓ cup white vinegar
1 shallot
6 black peppercorns
4 egg yolks
250g butter
½ cup mint leaves, firmly packed

Clockwise from left: Rack of Lamb with Mint Bearnaise; Lamb Curry; Cutlets Wellington; Stuffed Loin of Lamb; Ratatouille Lamb.

Trim excess fat from meat. Spread mustard over both sides of meat, brush with oil. Place meat in baking dish, bake in moderate oven 20 to 25 minutes. Serve with Mint Bearnaise.
Mint Bearnaise: Place vinegar, chopped shallot and peppercorns in pan, bring to boil, boil rapidly until reduced by half. Strain liquid into top of double saucepan, add egg yolks, beat over simmering water 1 minute. Add cooled melted butter, gradually continue beating until thickened. Remove from heat, place in blender with mint leaves, blend 30 seconds.
Serves 4.

LAMB CURRY
2½kg leg of lamb
½ teaspoon salt
1 tablespoon mild curry paste
1 teaspoon chilli powder
1 clove garlic
¼ cup brown vinegar
¼ teaspoon turmeric
60g ghee or butter
2 onions
3 cloves garlic, extra
1 teaspoon grated green ginger
1 teaspoon coriander
½ teaspoon cumin
3 cups water
2 beef stock cubes
1 tablespoon tomato paste
1 tablespoon cornflour
1 tablespoon water, extra

STUFFED LOIN OF LAMB
1 loin of lamb, containing 8 chops
⅓ cup bottled red currant jelly
1 tablespoon brandy
1 tablespoon oil
STUFFING
30g dried apricots
1 tablespoon fruit chutney
1 teaspoon green peppercorns
1 onion
45g butter
1 egg yolk
1 cup fresh breadcrumbs

Ask butcher to bone loin of lamb. Open loin of lamb, fat side down, on board, put prepared Stuffing along centre of lamb. Roll up, secure with string at 2.5cm intervals. Sprinkle oil into baking dish, add lamb, bake in moderate oven 1 to 1½ hours, basting regularly with combined melted jelly and brandy to give lamb a rich glaze. Serve hot or cold.

Stuffing: Melt butter in pan, add finely chopped onion, cook 1 minute, stir in finely chopped apricots, cook until onion is just tender. Remove from heat, stir in crushed green peppercorns and chutney; cool 5 minutes, stir in breadcrumbs and egg yolk.

Serves 4 to 6.

CUTLETS WELLINGTON
8 lamb cutlets
185g chicken liver pate
1 tablespoon chopped chives
8 mushrooms
8 sheets filo pastry
2 tablespoons oil
6 sprigs parsley
1 egg white
extra oil

Trim fat from cutlets. Heat oil in pan, add cutlets, cook until cutlets are cooked through, cool. Mash pate with chives, spread evenly over cutlets.

Slice each mushroom and arrange on top of cutlets.

Place a sheet of filo pastry on clean surface, brush with extra oil, fold in half vertically, brush with oil, then place cutlet to one side of pastry leaving a 5cm border on both sides. Fold pastry over cutlet, then roll up, tucking pastry in as you go to form a triangular parcel.

Brush with a little lightly beaten egg white, bake in moderately hot oven 12 to 15 minutes or until pastry is golden brown.

Serves 4.

Cut meat into 2.5cm cubes, place in bowl, add salt, curry paste, chilli powder, crushed garlic, vinegar and turmeric; stir until meat is coated. Cover, stand 30 minutes. Melt half the ghee in pan; when hot, add half the meat and stir until well browned; remove and place in bowl. Melt remaining ghee, add remaining meat and stir until browned; return all meat to pan. Add sliced onions, extra crushed garlic, ginger, coriander and cumin, cook stirring over medium heat 2 minutes. Pour into ovenproof dish, add water, crumbled stock cubes and tomato paste. Cover, bake in mod-

erate oven 1 hour. Cool, refrigerate overnight. Next day, remove any fat from top of curry. Pour curry into large pan, bring to boil, add blended cornflour and extra water, stir until sauce boils and thickens. Serve with fluffy boiled rice.

Serves 4.

Veal is popular because it has very little fat, and its subtle flavor will happily adopt tasty sauces and vegetables.

CRUSTY SAVORY VEAL CASSEROLE
125g butter
300g carton sour cream
1 egg
1 cup self-raising flour
pinch mixed herbs
½ cup cornflakes
60g cheddar cheese
FILLING
500g veal steak
60g butter
190g can whole mushrooms
1 carrot
1 green pepper
1 stick celery
1 onion
4 rashers bacon
400g can tomatoes
1 tablespoon chopped parsley

Combine soft butter, sour cream and egg in bowl, add sifted flour and herbs, mix until well combined. Spoon mixture into greased 2 litre ovenproof dish, work mixture up to cover sides and base of dish with spoon. Spoon in Filling, cover, bake in moderate oven 40 minutes or until crust is golden brown. Sprinkle combined crushed cornflakes and grated cheese over top of casserole, bake uncovered further 10 minutes.
Filling: Cut meat into 2.5cm cubes. Heat butter, add meat, cook until well browned. Add drained and halved mushrooms, diced carrot and diced pepper, chopped celery, chopped onion and chopped bacon, mix until combined. Stir in undrained mashed tomatoes and parsley, simmer gently uncovered 5 minutes.
Serves 4.

GLAZED SHOULDER OF VEAL
2½kg shoulder of veal
1 tablespoon brandy
2 tablespoons brown sugar
1 tablespoon honey
1 teaspoon grated lemon rind
1 tablespoon chopped parsley
¼ cup oil
¾ cup water
1½ tablespoons red currant jelly
1 tablespoon brandy, extra
1 tablespoon lemon juice
½ teaspoon cornflour
1 tablespoon water, extra

Combine brandy, brown sugar, honey, lemon rind and parsley in bowl. Place meat in baking dish, spread evenly with honey mixture, add oil. Bake in hot oven 15 minutes, reduce heat to moderate, bake further 1½ hours or until tender. Remove meat from baking dish, keep warm. Drain away excess oil, place baking dish over heat, stir in water, scraping in bits that cling to bottom of dish. Continue stirring until mixture boils. Strain mixture into a small pan. Add red currant jelly, extra brandy and lemon juice, mix until combined. Stir in blended cornflour and extra water, stir until sauce boils and thickens. Serve over sliced veal.
Serves 6.

VEAL AND MARSALA CASSEROLE
6 veal chops
flour
2 tablespoons oil
30g butter
1 onion
2 rashers bacon
2 tablespoons flour, extra
2 cups water
⅓ cup cream
2 tablespoons marsala
1 chicken stock cube
125g mushrooms
2 tablespoons chopped parsley

Coat chops lightly with flour. Heat butter and oil in large pan, add chops, brown well on both sides, remove from pan. Add peeled onion to pan with chopped bacon, cook until onion is transparent, remove from pan. Add extra flour to pan, stir until smooth, add water gradually, stir until sauce boils and thickens. Add cream, marsala, crumbled stock cube, chops and bacon mixture. Simmer covered 35 minutes, add sliced mushrooms, simmer covered further 10 minutes or until chops are tender. Add parsley just before serving.
Serves 4 to 6.

MOZZARELLA VEAL WITH FRESH TOMATO SAUCE
8 small veal steaks
4 slices mozzarella cheese
30g butter
2 tablespoons oil
30g butter, extra
1 onion
1 clove garlic
500g ripe tomatoes
1 tablespoon tomato paste
½ teaspoon sugar
1 chicken stock cube
¾ cup water
2 tablespoons chopped mint

Pound veal thinly, trim to even-sized oval shapes. Top 4 steaks with a slice of cheese to come to within 1cm of edge of veal all round. Top with remaining veal steaks, pressing edges firmly together. Heat butter and oil in pan, cook steaks slowly until golden brown and tender, remove from pan.

Melt extra butter in pan, add chopped onion and crushed garlic, cook until onion is transparent. Add chopped tomatoes and tomato paste. Add sugar, crumbled stock cube and water; bring to boil, reduce heat, simmer uncovered for 15 minutes, process or blend until smooth, push through strainer into pan, reheat, add mint. Spoon over veal.
Serves 4.

VEAL AND VEGETABLE CASSEROLE
1kg stewing veal
1 teaspoon paprika
30g butter
2 tablespoons oil
2 onions
1 clove garlic
400g can tomatoes
2 teaspoons brown sugar
1 teaspoon dry mustard
⅓ cup water
1 tablespoon dry white wine
1 beef stock cube
4 zucchini
90g mushrooms
440g can tiny potatoes
¼ cup sour cream
2 tablespoons chopped parsley

Chop meat into 2.5cm cubes, toss in paprika. Heat butter and oil in pan, brown meat well in batches, remove to ovenproof dish. Add chopped onions to pan and crushed garlic, cook until onions are transparent. Add undrained mashed tomatoes, sugar, mustard, water, wine and crumbled stock cube; bring to boil, reduce heat, simmer 10 minutes. Pour over meat, bake covered in moderate oven 1½ hours. Stir in chopped zucchini, sliced mushrooms, drained potatoes and sour cream. Cover, bake further 40 minutes or until meat is tender. Stir in chopped parsley just before serving.
Serves 4.

Clockwise from left: Crusty Savory Veal Casserole; Glazed Shoulder of Veal; Veal and Marsala Casserole; Mozzarella Veal with Fresh Tomato Sauce; Veal and Vegetable Casserole.

Subtle oriental flavors complement pork very well in this selection. Remember not to overcook pork; it should be moist and juicy.

PORK CHOPS PEKING STYLE
1kg pork chops
1cm piece green ginger
¼ teaspoon salt
½ teaspoon sesame oil
1 egg
2 teaspoons plain flour
2 teaspoons cornflour
1 teaspoon soy sauce
6 shallots
2 sticks celery
1 green pepper
oil for deep frying
SAUCE
1 clove garlic
3 tablespoons white vinegar
3 tablespoons tomato sauce
1 teaspoon lemon juice
2 tablespoons sugar
2 teaspoons dry sherry
2 teaspoons worcestershire sauce
¼ teaspoon chilli sauce

Remove skin from pork, cut pork into 5cm pieces. Grate ginger, squeeze juice from ginger (with fingers) over pork; discard ginger fibres. Add salt, sesame oil, half the lightly beaten egg, flours and the soy sauce; mix well, discard rest of egg. Cut shallots into 5cm lengths, add half the shallots to pork. Stand 1 hour. Remove shallots, discard. Chop celery and pepper into 2.5cm pieces. Heat oil, add pork in several batches, cook until golden brown; drain.

Reheat oil, return pork to oil and cook further 1 minute; drain. Pour off oil from pan, return pan to heat, add remaining shallots, celery, pepper and stir fry, 1 minute. Return pork to pan, add Sauce, stir fry 1 minute.
Sauce: Combine crushed garlic with remaining ingredients, mix well.

Serves 4.

PORK FILLETS WITH CURRY SAUCE
4 pork fillets (approx 250g each)
salt
2 tablespoons mango chutney
2 tablespoons oil
1 onion
2 tablespoons sultanas
1 teaspoon curry powder
1 teaspoon cornflour
¾ cup water

Remove any excess fat from fillets, rub with salt. Spread chutney evenly over fillets. Heat oil in baking dish, add fillets, cook over high heat until lightly browned on all sides. Then bake in moderately hot oven 20 to 25 minutes or until tender, brushing fillets once with pan drippings during cooking. Remove fillets from dish, slice, arrange on serving plate, keep warm. Add chopped onion to baking dish, cook until the onion is transparent. Add sultanas and curry powder, gradually stir in blended cornflour and water. Stir until sauce boils and thickens. Spoon over fillets.

Serves 6.

PORK FILLET WITH CELERY
500g pork fillet
1 clove garlic
3 teaspoons cornflour
½ teaspoon sugar
¼ teaspoon salt
1 teaspoon soy sauce
3 sticks celery
1 small carrot
¾ cup oil
SAUCE
1 tablespoon tomato sauce
½ teaspoon worcestershire sauce
2 tablespoons water
1 teaspoon sugar
¼ teaspoon salt
1 chicken stock cube
1 tablespoon hoi sin sauce
3 teaspoons barbecue sauce

Cut pork into 5mm slices. Combine crushed garlic, cornflour, sugar, salt and soy sauce in bowl, add meat, mix until combined, stand 20 minutes.

Slice celery diagonally, slice carrot thinly. Heat pan, add oil; when oil is hot, add meat, cook over high heat until golden brown. Add celery and carrot, cook further 1 minute, remove from pan. Drain excess oil from pan, add Sauce, stir over high heat until sauce boils and thickens. Add pork and vegetable mixture, mix well.
Sauce: Combine all ingredients.

Serves 4.

SPICY APRICOT SPARERIBS
1kg pork spareribs
425g can apricot nectar
½ cup white vinegar
2 teaspoons cornflour
2 teaspoons soy sauce
1 clove garlic
2 teaspoons grated green ginger
1 tablespoon mild chilli sauce
1 tablespoon hot water

Place ribs in pan, cover with water, add vinegar, bring to boil, boil uncovered 15 minutes, drain and rinse under cold water. Place ribs in shallow baking dish. Blend cornflour with soy sauce, lightly bruised peeled clove of garlic, apricot nectar, ginger and chilli sauce. Pour over spareribs, bake uncovered in moderate oven 1 hour. Place over heat on top of stove for 5 to 10 minutes, turn ribs until coated with sauce. Place ribs on serving plate; drain fat from pan, stir hot water into pan drippings, spoon over ribs.

Serves 4.

Clockwise from top right: Pork Fillets with Curry Sauce; Pork Chops Peking Style; Spicy Apricot Spareribs; Pork Fillet with Celery; Honey Glazed Loin of Pork.

HONEY GLAZED LOIN OF PORK

2kg loin of pork
½ teaspoon salt
pinch five spice powder
1 teaspoon salt, extra
2 tablespoons oil
⅓ cup honey
1½ tablespoons soy sauce
⅓ cup orange juice
1 teaspoon grated green ginger
1 teaspoon cornflour
2 tablespoons water
STUFFING
30g butter
2 shallots
1 stick celery
1 small green apple
2 cups fresh breadcrumbs
1 egg white

Ask butcher to bone pork and to score rind well. Open loin of pork, rind side down, on board. Combine salt with five spice powder, rub over inside of pork. Put prepared Stuffing along centre of pork. Roll up, secure with string at 2.5cm intervals. Rub extra salt and oil well into rind. Place in hot oven 10 to 15 minutes or until rind starts to crackle. Reduce heat to moderate, cook further 1 hour. Pour combined honey, soy sauce, orange juice and ginger over pork. Bake further 20 minutes, spooning sauce over occasionally until loin is cooked through.

Remove pork from baking dish, remove string, keep warm. Strain pan juices into a small pan, stand a few minutes then skim off all fat. Add blended cornflour and water, stir over heat until sauce boils and thickens.

Stuffing: Melt butter in pan, add chopped shallots and chopped celery, saute few minutes. Add peeled, cored and finely chopped apple, cook 1 minute, remove from heat. Mix in breadcrumbs and egg white.

Serves 8.

Here's a delicious selection of beef recipes, some with oriental flavor, plus a hearty casserole and two which are ideal for a barbecue.

GOURMET BEEF CASSEROLE
1kg blade steak
1 teaspoon brown sugar
salt, pepper
1 beef stock cube
1 tablespoon flour
pinch nutmeg
1 onion
2 cloves garlic
1 tablespoon vinegar
1 teaspoon worcestershire sauce
1 tablespoon tomato sauce
15g butter
1 tablespoon oil
1 tablespoon flour, extra
½ cup water
½ cup dry red wine
1 french bread stick
15g butter, extra
2 teaspoons french mustard

Cut meat into 2.5cm cubes. Combine sugar, salt and pepper, crumbled stock cube, flour, nutmeg, finely chopped onion, crushed garlic, vinegar, worcestershire sauce and tomato sauce. Spoon over meat, cover, leave to marinate 1 hour; stir occasionally.

Heat butter and oil in pan, add meat and marinade, cook 5 minutes. Place meat in ovenproof dish. Stir extra flour into pan drippings, cook 30 seconds. Stir in wine and water, stir until sauce boils and thickens. Pour sauce over meat, cover, bake in moderately slow oven 1¼ hours.

Cut bread stick into 2.5cm slices. Combine extra butter and mustard, spread on one side of bread slices. Places slices, mustard side up, on top of casserole, push down gently to soak up some of the sauce. Return to moderate oven, cook uncovered further 20 minutes or until top is brown and crisp.

Serves 4.

STEAK TERIYAKI
4 pieces fillet steak
2 tablespoons lemon juice
4 tablespoons teriyaki sauce
2 cloves garlic
1 teaspoon grated green ginger
½ cup pineapple juice
1½ tablespoons sugar
⅓ cup water
4 shallots
3 teaspoons cornflour
2 tablespoons oil

Combine lemon juice, teriyaki sauce, crushed garlic, ginger, pineapple juice, sugar and water in shallow dish, stir until sugar is dissolved. Trim steaks, flatten slightly, add to teriyaki mixture, stand 1 hour, turning steaks occasionally.

Drain steaks well, reserve teriyaki mixture. Heat oil in pan, add steaks, cook on both sides until done as desired, remove from pan, keep warm. Blend cornflour with teriyaki mixture, add to pan, stir over heat until sauce boils and thickens. Add chopped shallots, reduce heat, simmer 1 minute. Pour sauce over steaks.

Serves 4.

BEEF WITH PEPPERS AND PINEAPPLE
500g fillet steak, in one piece
450g can sliced pineapple
1 green pepper
1 red pepper
3 cloves garlic
1cm piece green ginger
3 shallots
2 tablespoons soy sauce
1 teaspoon sugar
2 teaspoons cornflour
2 tablespoons water
1½ tablespoons oil, extra
oil for frying
SAUCE
1 tablespoon oyster sauce
2 teaspoons soy sauce
1 teaspoon sugar
½ teaspoon sesame oil
1 teaspoon cornflour
¼ cup water

Remove any fat from meat. Cut meat into 3mm thick slices, place in bowl with soy sauce, sugar, cornflour and water; mix well. Stand 30 minutes.

Drain pineapple. Cut pineapple slices into quarters, cut peppers into 2.5cm cubes; cut shallots into 4cm lengths; slice ginger into wafer-thin slices. Heat oil in pan, add pineapple and peppers and stir fry over medium heat for 2 minutes, remove from pan.

Add extra oil to beef. Heat 2 tablespoons oil in pan, add garlic and ginger, cook until garlic turns golden brown. Add beef, spread out in pan; when brown on one side turn to brown other side. Cook quickly until meat just changes color; over-cooking will toughen meat. Remove from pan.

Sauce: Combine all ingredients in pan. When Sauce boils and thickens, add beef and vegetables, toss for 1 minute over high heat.

Serves 6.

SAVORY BEEF ROLLS
1kg rump steak
90g packaged cream cheese
½ teaspoon mixed herbs
flour
salt, pepper
15g butter
1 tablespoon oil
1 teaspoon soy sauce
½ cup beef stock
2 tablespoons cream
2 teaspoons chopped parsley

Combine cream cheese with pepper and herbs. Trim steak, cut into 8 pieces. Flatten each piece with meat mallet to approximately 12cm square. Spread cream cheese mixture evenly over steak, then roll up, secure with toothpicks.

Lightly coat steak rolls with flour seasoned with salt and pepper. Heat butter and oil in pan, add rolls in one layer, cook until evenly browned on all sides. Add combined soy sauce and stock. Bring to boil, reduce heat, simmer covered very gently 10 minutes or until cooked. Remove rolls from pan, remove toothpicks.

Place steak rolls on serving dish, keep warm. Boil stock in pan until reduced by half. Add cream and parsley. Pour over steak rolls.

Serves 4.

STEAK WITH PIQUANT BUTTER
6 pieces fillet or rump steak
1 onion
3 whole cloves
1 teaspoon peppercorns
1 bay leaf
½ teaspoon thyme
4 tablespoons oil
1¼ cups dry red wine
2 tablespoons oil
30g butter
PIQUANT BUTTER
1 teaspoon bottled horseradish cream
1 stick celery
½ teaspoon chopped capers
3 shallots
1 teaspoon sugar
125g butter

Place meat in china or glass dish. Slice onion, scatter over meat with cloves, peppercorns, bay leaf, thyme, oil and wine. Cover dish, refrigerate for several hours or overnight. Remove steaks from marinade, pat dry with kitchen paper. Heat oil and butter in pan, brown steaks on both sides, cook until done as desired. Serve topped with slice of piquant butter.

Piquant butter: Cream butter until soft, add horseradish cream, finely chopped celery, capers, finely chopped shallots and sugar. Place on a piece of foil and form into a sausage shape. Wrap in foil and refrigerate until firm.

Serves 6.

From back: Gourmet Beef Casserole; Savory Beef Rolls; Steak with Piquant Butter; Steak Teriyaki; Beef with Peppers and Pineapple.

Some miscellaneous super-special main course dishes; try the Cheesy Bacon and Egg Slice for breakfast, brunch, lunch, or a Sunday evening snack.

CHEESY BACON AND EGG SLICE

This is one of the tastiest and handiest recipes we have created in the kitchen. The whole dish is prepared, covered, refrigerated overnight and baked when you are ready the next day. It can be baked on the same day, but the flavor is not quite as good.

½ loaf unsliced white bread
125g grated cheddar cheese
5 rashers bacon
3 shallots
1 small green pepper
6 eggs
2 cups milk
1 teaspoon dry mustard
1 teaspoon worcestershire sauce
1 tablespoon mayonnaise
pepper
½ teaspoon dried basil leaves
1 small red pepper

Trim crusts from bread, cut bread into 2.5cm cubes, place bread in single layer in ovenproof dish. Sprinkle with cheese. Cut bacon in 2.5cm pieces, fry until crisp and brown, drain, place over cheese, top with chopped shallots and chopped green pepper.

Whisk eggs with fork, add milk, mustard, worcestershire sauce, mayonnaise, pepper and basil. Pour over bread mixture, top with chopped red pepper, cover with plastic food wrap, refrigerate overnight. Next day, bake uncovered in moderate oven for 50 to 60 minutes.
Serves 6.

VEGETABLE STRUDEL

1 eggplant
375g zucchini
1 onion
1 red pepper
250g mushrooms
60g butter
2 tablespoons tomato paste
2 tablespoons chopped parsley
¼ teaspoon thyme
salt, pepper
10 sheets filo pastry
2 tablespoons grated parmesan
    cheese
⅓ cup oil
CHEESE SAUCE
15g butter
2 teaspoons flour
1 cup milk
2 tablespoons grated parmesan
    cheese
30g cheddar cheese

Chop eggplant, zucchini, onion, red pepper and mushrooms into chunky pieces. Heat butter in large pan, add vegetables, toss in butter 2 minutes. Add tomato paste, chopped parsley, thyme, salt and pepper; stir to combine. Layer filo pastry sheets on top of each other, brush each sheet with oil. Spoon vegetable mixture down long edge of pastry, leaving approximately 5cm at each end. Roll up tightly, tuck ends under. Place on oven tray, brush top with oil, sprinkle with parmesan cheese. Bake in moderate oven 30 minutes or until lightly browned. Cut diagonally into slices to serve. Serve with Cheese Sauce.

Cheese Sauce: Heat butter in small pan, add flour, cook over heat 1 minute. Gradually add milk, stir over heat until sauce boils and thickens. Add grated cheeses, remove from heat, stir until cheese is melted.
Serves 6.

Clockwise from bottom left: Vegetable Strudel; Spaghetti and Mince Meat Casserole; Tripe with Mustard Sauce; Sausage and Bean Casserole; Cheesy Bacon and Egg Slice.

TRIPE WITH MUSTARD SAUCE
1kg honeycomb tripe
1 tablespoon lemon juice
30g butter
2 onions
2 rashers bacon
1 clove garlic
½ cup dry white wine
¾ cup water
1 beef stock cube
2 tablespoons french mustard
½ teaspoon oregano
2 sticks celery
1 red pepper
1 green pepper
125g mushrooms
salt, pepper
1 tablespoon chopped parsley
1 tablespoon cornflour
1 tablespoon water, extra

Place tripe in large pan with enough cold water to cover. Add lemon juice, bring slowly to boil, boil gently 5 minutes; drain well. Cut tripe into 5cm pieces. Melt butter in pan, add chopped onions, chopped bacon and crushed garlic, cook until onion is tender. Add wine, water, crumbled stock cube, mustard and oregano, stir until heated through. Place tripe and onion mixture in ovenproof dish; bake covered 1 hour or until tender. Add chopped celery, chopped peppers and the mushrooms to tripe. Season with salt and pepper. Stir in parsley and blended cornflour and extra water, bake further 10 to 15 minutes.
Serves 4.

SAUSAGE AND BEAN CASSEROLE
1kg thick sausages
310g can butter beans
300g can red kidney beans
2 onions
125g bacon pieces
455g can tomato soup
¼ cup water
1 green pepper
250g zucchini
1 tablespoon chopped parsley

Drain beans, rinse well under cold water, drain well. Cut onions into wedges. Fry or grill sausages until golden brown. Saute onion and chopped bacon pieces in pan until onion is transparent. Add beans, tomato soup and water, stir until mixture boils, add sausages. Reduce heat, simmer covered 15 minutes. Add chopped pepper and sliced zucchini, cover, cook further 5 minutes, stir in parsley.
Serves 4.

SPAGHETTI AND MINCE MEAT CASSEROLE
250g spaghetti
30g butter
1 onion
500g minced steak
440g can tomato puree
¼ teaspoon cinnamon
1 bay leaf
salt, pepper
½ cup grated parmesan cheese
SAUCE
60g butter
⅓ cup plain flour
2 cups milk

Cook spaghetti in large pan of boiling, salted water for 10 minutes; drain. Melt butter in pan, add chopped onion and meat, cook stirring over high heat for 5 minutes; pour off any surplus fat. Add tomato puree, cinnamon, bay leaf, salt and pepper, bring to boil, reduce heat, simmer covered 15 minutes. Discard bay leaf. Spread half the spaghetti over base of ovenproof dish, top with half the meat mixture, repeat layer of spaghetti and meat mixture. Pour Sauce over top, sprinkle with cheese. Bake uncovered in moderate oven for 30 minutes.
Sauce: Melt butter in pan, stir in flour, add milk, stir until sauce boils and thickens.
Serves 6.

VEGETABLE DISHES

Use these vegetable recipes to accompany meat, chicken, fish and so on, or serve the more substantial recipes as a main course in place of meat.

BROWN RICE RISOTTO
250g brown rice
1 red pepper
1 green pepper
2 sticks celery
1 onion
60g butter
4 cups hot water, approximately
1 chicken stock cube
2 tablespoons grated parmesan
  cheese
2 tablespoons chopped parsley

Finely chop peppers, celery and onion. Heat butter in pan, add onion, cook stirring until onion is transparent, add half the peppers and celery and all the rice. Stir in about one cup of the water, add crumbled stock cube, boil steadily, stirring until water is almost evaporated. Continue adding the hot water about a cup at a time and evaporating it until all water is used; stir often during cooking time.

Cooking time for a crunchy texture from the first addition of water is about 45 minutes. If a more tender rice is required, cook further, add more water until rice is as tender as desired. Stir in cheese, stir in remaining vegetables and parsley.

Serves 4.

TOMATO AND CHEESE PATTIES
1kg old potatoes
15g butter
2 tablespoons chopped parsley
salt, pepper
4 small firm tomatoes
1 tablespoon chopped fresh basil
125g mozzarella cheese
flour
2 eggs
packaged dry breadcrumbs
oil for deep-frying

Boil or steam potatoes until tender. Drain, mash well with butter, parsley, salt and pepper. Slice tomatoes (you will need 16 slices). Sprinkle basil, salt and pepper over tomato slices. Slice mozzarella cheese (you will need 8 cheese slices).

Place 1 slice of mozzarella cheese in between 2 slices of tomato. Mould warm potato around to seal the tomato and mozzarella cheese completely, shape into patties. Coat lightly with flour, dip in lightly beaten eggs, then breadcrumbs. Repeat the egg-and-breadcrumb process. Deep fry in hot oil until golden brown.

Makes 8.

SPINACH CHEESE SLICE
8 large spinach leaves
1 onion
250g feta cheese
125g cheddar cheese
pepper
5 eggs
6 sheets packaged filo pastry
60g butter

Wash and dry spinach, cut off white stalks, roll up leaves, shred finely. Combine spinach and finely chopped onion in bowl, stand 1 hour, drain off any excess liquid. Add crumbled feta cheese, finely grated cheddar cheese and pepper, mix well.

Fold each sheet of pastry to form a rough square; cover with greaseproof paper, then a damp cloth, stand until required. Place a piece of folded pastry in greased baking dish (base measures 23cm x 28cm). Brush with melted butter; repeat process with two more folded sheets, brush butter between each sheet.

Press spinach mixture firmly onto pastry. Beat eggs until frothy, pour evenly over spinach. Cover with remaining three folded sheets of pastry, brushing between each layer with melted butter. Brush top with melted butter.

Cut spinach slice into squares. Bake in moderate oven 45 minutes or until light golden brown. Serve hot.

BEAN AND VEGETABLE CASEROLE

310g can butter beans
60g butter
1 onion
1 clove garlic
½ red pepper
2 sticks celery
1 carrot
2 zucchini
¼ small cauliflower
125g green beans
4 shallots
400g can tomatoes
1 tablespoon chopped parsley
2 tablespoons chopped chives
1 teaspoon chopped mint
½ teaspoon dried basil
2 medium potatoes
½ cup grated cheddar cheese
15g butter, extra

Cut pepper into strips; slice celery, zucchini and beans; cut cauliflower into small flowerets; slice carrot, chop shallots. Heat butter in large pan, add chopped onion, cook until transparent. Add crushed garlic, celery, carrot, zucchini, pepper, cauliflower and beans. Stir over heat one minute. Add undrained mashed tomatoes, chives, mint and basil. Bring to boil stirring occasionally, remove from heat. Stir in drained and rinsed butter beans, shallots and parsley. Place vegetable mixture in ovenproof dish. Slice potatoes thinly, cover vegetables with single layer of potatoes, brush with extra melted butter, sprinkle with grated cheese. Bake uncovered in moderate oven 40 minutes or until potatoes are tender and golden brown.

Serves 6.

Left: Tomato and Cheese Patties; Brown Rice Risotto.
Above: Bean and Vegetable Casserole; Spinach and Cheese Slice.

BEETROOT WITH ORANGE

A 440g can small beetroot may be substituted for cooked beetroot in this recipe. If using canned beetroot, drain, heat through in the sauce.

500g beetroot
2 tablespoons brown sugar
1 tablespoon cornflour
15g butter
2 tablespoons vinegar
1 cup orange juice
1 tablespoon water

Cook beetroot in boiling salted water 50 to 60 minutes or until tender. Drain, peel, cut in slices or make small balls with a melon baller; set aside. Heat sugar, vinegar, strained orange juice and butter in pan. Blend cornflour with water, stir into the orange juice mixture, stir until mixture boils and thickens. Add beetroot, heat through.
   Serves 4.

MINTED TOMATOES AND CUCUMBER

1 cucumber
3 tomatoes
2 tablespoons oil
1 tablespoon lemon juice
1 clove garlic
1 tablespoon chopped parsley
2 tablespoons grated parmesan cheese
1 tablespoon chopped mint

Peel cucumber, slice thinly. Slice tomatoes thinly. Arrange overlapping slices of tomato and cucumber alternately in heatproof dish. Combine oil, lemon juice, crushed garlic and parsley. Pour mixture over tomato and cucumber. Sprinkle with cheese, cook under hot griller until cheese melts; sprinkle with mint.
   Serves 4 to 6.

CREAMY CAMEMBERT POTATOES

750g old potatoes
2 tablespoons sour cream
15g butter
1 clove garlic
125g can camembert cheese
salt, pepper
2 tablespoons chopped chives

Boil or steam potatoes in usual way until tender; drain. Mash potatoes with sour cream until smooth. Remove rind from cheese, chop cheese roughly. Melt butter in pan, add crushed garlic and cheese, stir over low heat until cheese melts, add to potato. Season with salt and pepper, stir through chives. Serve hot.
   Serves 4.

Clockwise from top left: Potatoes and Caviar; Minted Tomatoes and Cucumber; Cauliflower with Crumb Topping; Garlic Tomato Beans; Beetroot with Orange; Corn and Bacon-Stuffed Tomatoes; Creamy Camembert Potatoes; Italian Broad Bean Salad.

CORN AND BACON-STUFFED TOMATOES

4 tomatoes
30g butter
2 shallots
1 clove garlic
2 rashers bacon
130g can corn kernels
⅓ cup fresh breadcrumbs
¼ cup grated cheese

Slice off about 2.5cm from top of each tomato. Scoop out tomato pulp carefully with teaspoon, chop pulp finely. Chop bacon finely, fry in pan until crisp, drain. Add butter, chopped shallots and crushed garlic, cook 1 minute, add drained corn, breadcrumbs, cheese and tomato pulp.

Spoon filling into tomatoes, stand tomatoes in ovenproof dish, bake in moderate oven 20 minutes.

Serves 4.

GARLIC TOMATO BEANS

500g green beans
4 tomatoes
1 onion
2 tablespoons pine nuts
30g butter
1 clove garlic
1 tablespoon oil
½ teaspoon dried basil
salt, pepper

String and slice beans; slice onion; peel and chop tomatoes. Melt butter in pan, add pine nuts and crushed garlic, cook until nuts are golden brown; remove from pan, drain on absorbent paper. Add oil to pan drippings, stir in onion, cook until just tender; add beans, cook further 2 minutes, then stir in tomatoes and basil. Cover, simmer gently 3 minutes or until beans are just cooked. Season with salt and pepper.

Serves 6.

ITALIAN BROAD BEAN SALAD

1kg broad beans
salt, pepper
1 clove garlic
2 tablespoons oil
2 teaspoons lemon juice
1 small stick celery
1 small onion
1 tablespoon chopped parsley

Shell beans, boil or steam in usual way for about 10 minutes until just tender (the outside husk of the shelled bean can be removed after cooking). Place drained hot beans in basin, season with salt, add crushed garlic, oil and lemon juice, toss lightly, cool to room temperature. Add finely chopped celery, peeled and sliced onion and parsley, season with pepper.

Serves 4.

POTATOES AND CAVIAR

5 potatoes
30g butter
3 shallots
60g packaged cream cheese
2 tablespoons cream
salt, pepper
½ cup sour cream
60g red or black caviar

Scrub unpeeled potatoes, rub with salt. Bake potatoes in moderately hot oven until just tender, approximately 1 hour. Remove potatoes from oven, cut tops from potatoes, carefully scoop out potato, mash well. Heat butter in pan, add chopped shallots, cook 1 minute. Add to mashed potato with cream cheese, cream, salt and pepper, mix well.

Spoon or pipe potato mixture back into four of the potato shells, place in ovenproof serving dish, cover with aluminium foil, bake in moderate oven 30 minutes. Top each potato with a tablespoon of sour cream and a spoonful of caviar.

Serves 4.

CAULIFLOWER WITH CRUMB TOPPING

1 small cauliflower
¼ cup cream
15g butter
1 clove garlic
TOPPING
2 eggs, separated
¼ cup milk
¼ cup cream
½ cup fresh breadcrumbs
½ teaspoon dry mustard
salt, pepper
½ cup grated cheese

Cut cauliflower into flowerets or leave whole if desired. Boil or steam until just tender; drain. Place cauliflower in ovenproof dish. Heat cream in pan, add butter and crushed garlic, pour over cauliflower. Spoon Topping over; stand dish in baking dish with hot water to come halfway up the sides, bake in moderate oven 25 minutes or until golden brown.

Topping: Combine egg yolks, milk, cream, breadcrumbs, mustard, salt, pepper and cheese in bowl; mix well. Beat egg whites until soft peaks form, fold half the whites into breadcrumb mixture, then gently fold in remaining egg whites.

Serves 4 to 6.

ZUCCHINI SLICE
375g zucchini
1 large onion
3 rashers bacon
1 cup grated cheddar cheese
1 cup self-raising flour
½ cup oil
5 eggs
salt, pepper

Grate unpeeled zucchini coarsely, finely chop onion and bacon. Combine zucchini, onion, bacon, cheese, sifted flour, oil and lightly beaten eggs, season with salt and pepper. Pour into well-greased lamington tin (base measures 16cm × 26cm), bake in moderate oven 30 to 40 minutes or until browned.

Serves 4 to 6.

CRUNCHY VEGETABLE FLAN
½ × 250g packet sesame biscuits
½ cup wheatgerm
125g butter
1 onion
250g zucchini (about 4)
salt, pepper
185g mushrooms
1 teaspoon dried marjoram
¼ teaspoon dried tarragon leaves
1 cup grated cheddar cheese
½ cup grated parmesan cheese
2 eggs
⅓ cup milk
1 tomato

Crush biscuits finely, mix with ¼ cup of the wheatgerm and 90g of the melted butter. Press over sides and base of 23cm flan tin. Bake in moderately hot oven 8 minutes or until golden brown. Remove from oven and set aside. Peel and slice onion, chop zucchini, slice mushrooms. Cook in remaining butter until tender, about 3 minutes. Mix in remaining wheatgerm, salt, pepper, marjoram and tarragon.

Turn half the filling into crumb shell. Sprinkle with half the cheeses. Top with remaining vegetable mixture. Beat eggs with milk; pour into centre of vegetable mixture. Arrange slices of tomato on top of vegetables; sprinkle with remaining cheeses. Bake in moderate oven 30 minutes or until set.

Serves 6.

VEGETARIAN POTATO KUGEL
3 medium potatoes
2 small carrots
1 small onion
1 clove garlic
1 egg
1 tablespoon oil
2 tablespoons chopped parsley
2 tablespoons wholemeal bread crumbs
½ cup milk powder
½ cup grated tasty cheese
15g butter
½ cup plain yoghurt
2 shallots

Grate potatoes, carrots and onion, combine with crushed garlic. Lightly beat egg with oil, pour over grated vegetables, stir in chopped parsley, breadcrumbs and milk powder. Spread into well greased pie dish (base measures 20cm), dot with buter, bake in moderate oven 30 minutes, sprinkle with cheese, bake further 15 minutes. Serve hot or cold topped with combined yoghurt and chopped shallots.

Serves 4 to 6.

Left: Zucchini Slice.
Above: Vegetarian Potato Kugel;
Crunchy Vegetable Flan.

FRUIT CAKES

We've selected our most often requested fruit cakes. They are all different – some are suitable for making the whole year round; the richer ones are ideal for Christmas, weddings, 21st birthdays and so on. Fruit cakes will keep and cut best if stored in the refrigerator. They will all freeze successfully for several months, though there is no need to freeze the richer cakes.

GRAND MARNIER FRUIT CAKE
500g sultanas
250g mixed peel
125g raisins
125g dates
125g prunes
125g glace apricots
125g glace pineapple
60g blanched slivered almonds
60g walnut pieces
1 tablespoon grated orange rind
½ cup Grand Marnier
½ cup castor sugar
¼ cup orange juice
250g butter
½ cup brown sugar, firmly packed
5 eggs
2 cups plain flour

Place sultanas and peel in large basin, chop all fruit the same size as a sultana and add to the basin. Mix in almonds, walnuts and orange rind. Sprinkle castor sugar evenly into heavy based pan, place over medium heat, cook until sugar is beginning to melt and brown, gently stir sugar until completely melted and golden brown. Remove from heat, add orange juice, return to heat, stir constantly until toffee pieces are dissolved. Do not boil mixture; this will evaporate too much of the liquid. Add Grand Marnier, strain to remove any small pieces of toffee; cool.

Place fruit mixture in airtight container or large jar which has tight fitting screw-top, pour Grand Marnier mixture over fruit mixture. Seal with plastic lid, stand overnight. Next day, invert jar or mix fruit mixture well. Do this for 10 days.

Beat butter until soft, add brown sugar, beat until combined. Add eggs one at a time, beat only until combined before adding the next egg. Pour fruit mixture into large basin, add creamed mixture, mix well; use your hand for most efficient mixing. Add sifted flour; mix well.

Prepare a deep 20cm square or deep 23cm round cake tin by lining base and sides with three thicknesses of greaseproof paper. Bring lining paper 5cm above edge of tin. Spread mixture evenly into tin, bake in slow oven 3 to 3½ hours. Brush top evenly with about 2 tablespoons extra Grand Marnier, cover with aluminium foil, leave until cold before removing from tin. To store cake: remove foil and tin, do not remove lining paper, wrap cake securely in plastic food wrap to make airtight, store in cool dark place, preferably in refrigerator. This cake will keep for at least a year.

To decorate cake with Marzipan Oranges: Buy a packet of almond paste from a health food store (some supermarkets stock it). Dust hands well with sifted pure icing sugar. Roll pieces of paste into balls, place small part of clove in position on orange. Use skewer to roll orange gently over grater to give effect of orange skin. Stand oranges on wire rack to dry overnight. Paint with orange food coloring, leave to dry overnight. Arrange oranges with fresh or artificial holly and toasted almonds on top of cake.

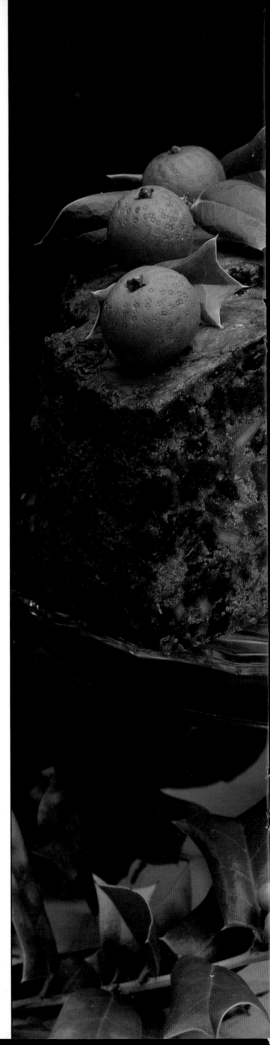

Grand Marnier Fruit Cake is a rich, elegant recipe ideal for a festive occasion.

CELEBRATION CAKE
500g sultanas
250g raisins
250g dates
125g currants
125g mixed peel
125g glace cherries
60g glace pineapple
60g glace apricots
½ cup rum, brandy, whisky or sherry
250g butter
1 cup brown sugar, firmly packed
5 eggs
1½ cups plain flour
⅓ cup self-raising flour
1 teaspoon mixed spice

Chop raisins, dates, peel, cherries, pineapple and apricots the same size as sultanas; combine in large basin with sultanas, currants and rum; mix well. Cover, stand overnight or up to a week. Line a deep 20cm square or deep 23cm round cake tin with three thicknesses of greaseproof paper; bring paper 5cm above edges of tin.

Beat butter until soft; add sugar; beat only until combined. Add eggs one at a time, beating well after each addition. Add creamed mixture to fruit mixture; mix well. Stir in sifted dry ingredients; mix thoroughly. Spread evenly into prepared tin; bake in slow oven 3 to 3½ hours. When cooked, brush evenly with about 2 tablespoons extra rum. Cover tightly with aluminium foil; leave until cold. Remove foil and tin, leave lining paper intact. Wrap in plastic food wrap. Store for up to a year in refrigerator.

FESTIVE FRUIT AND NUT CAKE
250g dates
125g glace pineapple
125g glace apricots
125g red glace cherries
125g green glace cherries
125g whole blanched almonds
250g brazil nuts
2 eggs
½ cup brown sugar, lightly packed
1 tablespoon rum
90g butter
⅓ cup plain flour
3 tablespoons self-raising flour

Chop pineapple and apricots into fairly large pieces; leave remaining fruit and nuts whole. Mix all well together. Beat eggs until thick and creamy, add sugar, vanilla, rum and soft butter, beating until combined. Stir in sifted flours and fruit and nut mixture.

Divide mixture between 2 greased bar tins (base measures 7cm x 25cm) with base lined with greaseproof paper. Press mixture firmly into tins. Bake in slow oven 1¼ hours or until cake is firm to touch; cool in tin 10 minutes. When cold, wrap in plastic food wrap and refrigerate in airtight container for at least 3 months.

RUSSIAN CHRISTMAS CAKE (MAZURKA)

This is a very slender cake, quite different from our traditional Christmas cake. It is ideal for those who do not like a hearty, rich fruit cake.

125g currants
125g sultanas
125g raisins
125g dates
125g figs
125g blanched almonds
125g mixed peel
60g glace cherries
60g glace pineapple
3 eggs
⅓ cup honey
1¼ cups plain flour

Combine currants and sultanas in basin, chop all other fruit and almonds the same size as sultanas, add to basin with lightly beaten eggs, honey and sifted flour. Mix well until ingredients are combined thoroughly. Press mixture evenly over base of greased and lined swiss roll tin (base measures 25cm x 30cm), bake in slow oven for 1 hour, cool in tin. Cut when cold. Store in airtight container, refrigerated, for up to a month.

RICH BOILED FRUIT CAKE
750g mixed fruit
250g dates
125g glace cherries
125g butter
¾ cup brown sugar, firmly packed
1 teaspoon mixed spice
½ cup water
½ cup sherry
2 eggs
2 tablespoons marmalade
1 cup self-raising flour
1 cup plain flour

Line a deep 20cm round cake tin with two thicknesses of greaseproof paper, bringing paper 5cm above edge of tin.

Chop mixed fruit and dates, halve cherries; combine in pan with butter, sugar, spice and water. Stir over heat until butter is melted; bring to boil; boil uncovered 3 minutes. Remove from heat, allow to become completely cold.

Add sherry, eggs and marmalade; mix well. Add sifted flours, mix well; spread evenly into prepared tin, bake in moderately slow oven about 2 hours. Cover with aluminium foil, cool in tin. Remove foil and tin, leave lining paper intact, refrigerate in plastic food wrap for up to a month.

Clockwise from top: Russian Christmas Cake; Rich Boiled Fruit Cake; Festive Fruit and Nut Cake; Celebration Cake.

GOLDEN FRUIT CAKE

Golden Fruit Cake is a rich, buttery, light cake, ideal for the festive season and a nice change from the traditional style of fruit cake.

250g sultanas
125g mixed peel
60g slivered almonds
125g glace cherries
125g glace pineapple
125g glace apricots
125g glace ginger
250g butter
1 teaspoon grated lemon rind
1 cup castor sugar
4 eggs
1½ cups plain flour

Line a deep, 20cm round cake tin with three layers of greaseproof paper, bringing paper 5cm above edge of tin. Combine sultanas, peel and almonds in bowl, add chopped glace fruit. Cream butter, lemon rind and sugar; beat in eggs one at a time. Stir into fruit mixture, then stir in sifted flour. Spread mixture evenly in tin, decorate top with almonds if desired. Bake in slow oven for 3 hours or until cooked when tested.

Cool, covered in tin. When cold, refrigerate in airtight container for up to 3 months.

BOILED PINEAPPLE FRUIT CAKE

470g can crushed pineapple
500g mixed fruit
125g butter
1 cup sugar
1 teaspoon mixed spice
1 teaspoon bicarbonate of soda
2 eggs
1 cup plain flour
1 cup self-raising flour

Line deep 20cm round cake tin with two thicknesses of greaseproof paper, bringing paper 5cm above edges of tin. Combine undrained pineapple, chopped fruit, butter, sugar, spice and soda in pan. Stir over heat until sugar is dissolved, bring to boil; boil uncovered 3 minutes. Allow to become cold. When cold, add eggs and sifted flours, mix well. Spread into prepared tin. Bake in moderately slow oven 1½ to 2 hours.

Cover, leave in tin until completely cold. Remove from tin, leave lining paper intact. Refrigerate in airtight container for up to a week.

MELT-AND-MIX FRUIT CAKE

1½kg mixed fruit
½ cup sherry, rum, whisky or brandy
1 Granny Smith apple
1 tablespoon honey or golden syrup
1 cup brown sugar, firmly packed
250g butter
4 eggs
1½ cups plain flour
½ cup self-raising flour
1 teaspoon mixed spice

Place chopped mixed fruit in large basin, add sherry, peeled and coarsely grated apple, honey, sugar and eggs; mix well with wooden spoon or hand to break up any large clumps of fruit. Add cooled, melted butter, sifted flours and spice; mix thoroughly. Place in deep 23cm round or deep 20cm square cake tin lined with three sheets of greaseproof paper. Bring paper 5cm above edge of tin.

Bake in slow oven 3½ hours or until cooked when tested. Remove from oven, brush evenly with about 2 tablespoons of extra sherry, cover tightly with aluminium foil, leave until cold. Remove from tin, leaving lining paper intact. Refrigerate in plastic food wrap for at least 6 months.

From left: Golden Fruit Cake; Boiled Pineapple Fruit Cake; Melt-and-Mix Fruit Cake.

Here are some old and new favorites of yours and ours: homely recipes, ideal for afternoon tea with family and friends.

LEMON SOUR CREAM CAKE
250g butter
2 teaspoons grated lemon rind
2¼ cups castor sugar
6 eggs
¼ cup self-raising flour
2 cups plain flour
¾ cup sour cream

Cream butter, lemon rind and sugar until light and fluffy. Beat in eggs, one at a time. Stir in sifted dry ingredients alternately with sour cream.

Spread mixture into greased deep 23cm round cake tin or well greased fancy ring tin, as shown, which has base lined with greased greaseproof paper. Bake in moderately slow oven 1½ to 1¾ hours.

WALNUT COFFEE CAKE
125g butter
1 teaspoon vanilla
¾ cup castor sugar
1 egg
½ cup sour cream
¾ cup plain flour
2 tablespoons self-raising flour
125g walnuts
1 tablespoon castor sugar, extra
½ teaspoon cinnamon

Cream butter, vanilla, sugar and egg until light and fluffy, stir in sour cream, then sifted flours in two batches. Spread half the mixture over base of loaf tin (base measures 9cm x 22cm) which has base lined with greased greaseproof paper, sprinkle evenly with half the combined chopped walnuts, extra sugar and cinnamon. Spread remaining cake mixture on top, sprinkle with remaining walnut mixture. Bake in moderate oven 45 minutes.

Stand few minutes before turning onto wire rack to cool.

Lemon Sour Cream Cake (top); Walnut Coffee Cake.

73

ALMOND BUTTER CAKE
250g butter
2 cups plain flour
4 eggs
1 cup castor sugar
1 teaspoon baking powder
1 tablespoon plain flour, extra
90g ground almonds
30g flaked almonds

Cream butter and flour in large bowl of electric mixer until light and fluffy. Beat eggs and sugar in small bowl until thick and creamy. Sift baking powder and extra flour together, add ground almonds, fold into egg mixture alternately with creamed butter mixture. Spread into deep well-greased 20cm round cake tin, smooth top, sprinkle with flaked almonds. Bake in slow oven approximately 2 hours.

APRICOT AND WALNUT LOAF
185g dried apricots
1 cup water
2 cups self-raising flour
½ teaspoon bicarbonate of soda
⅔ cup castor sugar
1 tablespoon grated orange rind
90g walnuts
⅓ cup orange juice
1 egg
60g butter

Place chopped apricots and water in pan, bring to boil, reduce heat, simmer covered until tender (about 5 minutes), drain; reserve ¼ cup of the liquid. Cool apricots to room temperature. Sift flour, soda and sugar into bowl, add apricots, orange rind and chopped walnuts.

Combine orange juice, egg, melted butter and reserved apricot liquid together; add to dry ingredients; mix well. Spoon into greased loaf tin (base measures 11cm x 18cm) lined with greaseproof paper, bake in moderately slow oven 50 to 60 minutes.

Stand in tin 5 minutes before turning on to wire rack to cool. Serve warm or cold, sliced with butter.

GINGER CAKE
125g butter
½ cup brown sugar, firmly packed
2 eggs
1 cup golden syrup
⅓ cup sultanas
60g glace ginger
2 cups plain flour
1 teaspoon ground ginger
½ cup milk
½ teaspoon bicarbonate of soda

Cream butter and sugar, beat until light and fluffy, beat in eggs one at a time. Fold in golden syrup, sultanas, chopped ginger and sifted flour and ground ginger. Warm milk, add soda. Stir immediately into cake mixture. Pour into greased lamington tin (base measures 16cm x 26cm), bake in moderately slow oven 1 hour.

BOILED DATE CAKE
185g butter
1 cup milk
½ cup brown sugar, firmly packed
1 cup finely chopped dates
½ teaspoon bicarbonate of soda
2 eggs
2¼ cups self-raising flour

Combine butter, milk, sugar and chopped dates in pan, stir over heat until butter is melted, bring to boil, remove from heat, stir in soda, stand 5 minutes. Stir in lightly beaten eggs and sifted flour in two lots, mix well. Pour mixture into well-greased 20cm ring tin, bake in moderate oven 40 minutes. Turn onto wire rack to cool. Serve buttered.

SULTANA CHERRY CAKE
⅓ cup sugar
⅓ cup water
250g butter
2 teaspoons glycerine
1 teaspoon vanilla
2 cups plain flour
4 eggs
¾ cup castor sugar
500g sultanas
185g glace cherries
60g mixed peel
¾ cup self-raising flour

Combine sugar and water in pan, stir over heat until sugar is dissolved, bring to boil. Remove syrup from heat, cool. Cream butter with glycerine and vanilla in large basin of electric mixer until butter is as white as possible. Add sifted plain flour, beat on low speed until combined. Increase speed slightly, beat 3 minutes or until mixture is smooth and creamy. Beat eggs and castor sugar in small basin of electric mixer until mixture is thick and sugar dissolved.

Add half the egg mixture to butter and flour mixture, beat on low speed until combined. Add remaining egg mixture, beat only until combined. Stir in sultanas, halved cherries and peel, then sifted self-raising flour with cold syrup. Spread mixture into greased and greased paper-lined deep 23cm round or deep 20cm square cake tin. Bake in slow oven 2½ hours, or until cooked when tested. Leave in tin until cake is cold.

Clockwise from left: Apricot and Walnut Loaf; Almond Butter Cake; Ginger Cake; Sultana Cherry Cake; Boiled Date Cake.

BUTTERSCOTCH CAKE
250g butter
1 teaspoon vanilla
1 cup brown sugar, lightly packed
2 eggs, separated
1 tablespoon golden syrup
1 cup self-raising flour
½ cup plain flour
½ teaspoon cinnamon
½ cup milk
CARAMEL ICING
60g butter
½ cup brown sugar, lightly packed
¾ cup icing sugar
¼ cup milk

Cream butter, vanilla and sugar until light and fluffy, beat in egg yolks and golden syrup, beat until well combined. Fold in sifted flour and cinnamon alternately with milk. Beat egg whites until soft peaks form, fold gently into mixture. Spread mixture into greased deep 20cm (8in) round cake tin which has base lined with greased greaseproof paper. Bake in moderate oven 50 to 60 minutes. Turn onto wire rack to cool. When cake is cold, top with Caramel Icing.

Caramel Icing: Melt butter in saucepan, add sugar, stir over medium heat 3 minutes, gradually add milk, stir until sauce boils; remove from heat, leave to become cold. Gradually add sifted icing sugar, beat until thick and spreadable.

HIGH-RISE BUTTER CAKE
¾ cup sugar
⅓ cup water
125g butter
1 teaspoon vanilla
3 eggs, separated
1½ cups self-raising flour

Combine sugar and water in pan, stir over heat without boiling until sugar is dissolved, bring to boil, remove from heat, cool syrup to room temperature.

Beat butter, vanilla and egg yolks together until light and creamy. With mixer on medium speed, gradually pour in syrup in a thin stream, continue beating until all syrup is mixed in. Transfer mixture to a larger basin. Stir in sifted flour all at once. Beat egg whites until soft peaks form, fold half the egg whites through mixture, then fold remaining egg whites gently through mixture.

Spread into well-greased deep 20cm round cake tin, bake in moderate oven 40 minutes. Stand few minutes before turning onto wire rack to cool.

VARIATIONS
Caramel: Substitute brown sugar for white; pack sugar firmly into cup.
Wholemeal: Substitute half the white self-raising flour for wholemeal self-raising flour (return husks fom sifter to mixture). If desired, raw sugar can be substituted for white sugar; it will take a little longer to dissolve.
Sultana, Cherry or Date: Stir in 125g chopped fruit before the flour is added, chop any added fruit the same size as a sultana.
Coconut: Add ⅓ cup coconut to the hot syrup, cool as above.
Lemon, Orange: Omit vanilla and add 2 teaspoons grated rind to butter and egg yolk mixture. Squeeze juice from fruit, measure and, if necessary, add more water to make up to the amount of liquid specified above.
Coffee: Dissolve 1 tablespoon instant coffee powder in the water before adding sugar.
Chocolate: Blend 2 tablespoons sifted cocoa with the hot syrup.
Apple: Spread two-thirds of the cake mixture into tin, top evenly with half 425g can of dessert apple, spread with remaining cake mixture. Apple cakes will take 5 to 10 minutes longer to cook than other variations, due to the moistness of the apple.
Glace Icing: Sift 1½ cups icing sugar into basin, add 1 teaspoon soft or melted butter, blend to smooth paste with 1 to 2 tablespoons liquid. Use orange or lemon juice, milk or water to correspond with flavor of cake.

Stir over hot water until of spreading consistency and spread evenly over cold cake.

Chocolate Icing: Add 2 tablespoons sifted cocoa to icing sugar.
Coffee icing: Dissolve 1 to 2 teaspoons instant coffee powder in liquid to be added to icing.

This cake mixture can be cooked in any of the following sized tins; cooking times depend on size of tin.
Loaf tins: 40 to 50 minutes.
Lamington tin (base measures 16cm x 26cm): 30 minutes.
2 Bar tins (base measures 7cm x 25cm): 30 minutes.
Baba or ring tin (20cm): 35 to 40 minutes.
Patty pans: 10 to 15 minutes.

COCONUT ORANGE CAKE
½ cup coconut
½ cup milk
125g butter
1 cup castor sugar
1 tablespoon grated orange rind
2 eggs
1½ cups self-raising flour
½ cup milk, extra
ORANGE ICING
1½ cups icing sugar
1 teaspoon soft butter
1½ tablespoons orange juice, approx

Combine coconut and milk in bowl, stand 1 hour.

Cream butter, sugar and orange rind until light and fluffy. Beat in eggs one at a time. Stir in sifted flour, coconut mixture and extra milk alternately (mixture will appear curdled at this stage); pour into greased loaf tin (base measures 11cm x 18cm) with base lined with greaseproof paper. Bake in moderate oven 50 to 60 minutes.

Stand 5 minutes, turn onto wire rack. Top with Orange Icing, cool.
Orange Icing: Sift icing sugar into bowl, add butter and enough orange juice to mix to a smooth paste.

APPLE CINNAMON CAKE
4 green apples
1 cup brown sugar, lightly packed
1 cup water
125g butter
½ cup castor sugar
2 eggs
2 cups self-raising flour
1 teaspoon cinnamon
½ cup milk

Peel, core and quarter apples, cut into 1cm slices. Put apples, brown sugar and water in pan, stir until sugar has dissolved. Bring to boil, reduce heat, simmer uncovered until apples are just tender (about 7 minutes). Drain apples, reserve syrup.

Cream butter and sugar until light and fluffy. Beat in eggs, one at a time. Fold in sifted flour and cinnamon alternately with milk. Spread half the cake mixture evenly over base of greased 23cm springform tin, top with half the apple. Spread remaining cake mixture evenly over apple layer. Arrange remaining apples decoratively over top. Bake in moderate oven 50 minutes to 1 hour. Boil reserved syrup rapidly until reduced to about half. Brush top of cake with hot syrup. Serve cold as a cake or warm as a dessert with cream or custard.

From back: Butterscotch Cake; Coconut Orange Cake; Plain High-Rise Butter Cake; Coffee High-Rise Butter Cake; Apple High-Rise Butter Cake.

DUNDEE CAKE

250g butter
1 cup brown sugar, firmly packed
5 eggs
375g raisins
60g mixed peel
60g glace cherries
60g ground almonds
1 tablespoon honey
1 tablespoon rum or orange juice
2 cups plain flour
½ cup self-raising flour
60g slivered almonds

Cream butter and sugar until combined, beat in eggs one at a time. Stir in chopped raisins, peel and halved cherries, add ground almonds, honey and rum; mix well. Stir in sifted flours. Spread mixture into greased and greased paper-lined deep 20cm round cake tin or loaf tin (base measures 12cm x 22cm), sprinkle evenly with slivered almonds. Bake in moderately slow oven for 2 to 2½ hours, cool cake in tin.

DUTCH GINGER CAKE

1¾ cups plain flour
1 cup castor sugar
125g glace ginger
1 egg
185g butter
30g blanched almonds

Sift flour, add sugar and chopped ginger, mix in melted butter and egg.

Press mixture into well greased 20cm sandwich tin. Brush top with a little milk, decorate with almonds. Bake in moderate oven 45 minutes, cool in tin, cut into wedges to serve.

HONEY SPONGE

This lightly textured sponge contains no water or milk.

3 large eggs
½ cup honey
1 cup self-raising flour
300ml jar thickened cream

Beat whole eggs on high speed in small basin of electric mixer until eggs are thick and creamy (this will take up to 5 minutes). Add honey in a thin stream gradually to eggs while they are still beating, continue beating on high speed for further 5 minutes. Transfer mixture to large basin, sift flour over egg mixture, fold in lightly with spatula, knife or hand (use one hand with fingers outstretched to combine ingredients). Spread mixture into well-greased lamington tin (base measures 16cm x 26cm), bake in moderate oven 25 minutes or until sponge feels firm to touch and is slightly shrunken from sides of tin. Turn onto wire rack to cool. When cold, split in half, fill with whipped cream, dust top with sifted icing sugar.

ALMOND APRICOT CAKE

⅔ cup self-raising flour
⅔ cup plain flour
125g butter
¼ cup castor sugar
1 teaspoon vanilla
1 tablespoon milk
⅓ cup apricot jam
TOPPING
3 eggs, separated
2 teaspoons warm water
⅓ cup sugar
1 teaspoon vanilla
2 tablespoons self-raising flour
2 tablespoons cornflour
90g ground almonds
60g butter

Sift flours, rub in butter, add sugar, vanilla and milk, mix to a soft dough. Place on lightly floured surface, knead lightly until smooth, cover, refrigerate 30 minutes. Cut two thirds from pastry, press evenly over base of wel-greased lamington tin (base measures 16cm x 26cm); return remaining dough to refrigerator while preparing Topping.

Spread pastry in tin with apricot jam. Spread Topping evenly over jam, then roll remaining pastry to rectangular shape on floured surface, cut into 1cm strips, decorate top by placing strips in a lattice pattern. Bake in moderate oven 30 to 40 minutes. Cool in tin before cutting.

Topping: Beat egg yolks, water, sugar and vanilla on electric mixer until thick and creamy, transfer to large basin. Beat egg whites until soft peaks form, place on top of egg yolk mixture, sift flour and cornflour on top of egg whites, add almonds, fold all ingredients together very gently, then fold in melted butter.

Clockwise from bottom left: Dutch Ginger Cake; Dundee Cake; Apple Cinnamon Cake; Honey Sponge; Almond Apricot Cake.

BANANA WALNUT CAKE

125g butter
¾ cup castor sugar
2 eggs
3 very ripe, small bananas
1 teaspoon vanilla
½ cup chopped walnuts
¾ cup self-raising flour
¾ cup plain flour
1 teaspoon bicarbonate of soda

Mash bananas finely with fork (you should have ¾ cup mashed banana). Cream butter and sugar until light and fluffy. Add eggs one at a time, beating well after each addition. Add bananas and vanilla, beat on low speed until well combined. Stir in walnuts, then sifted flours and soda in two lots; mix well. Spread mixture into well-greased 20cm ring tin, bake in moderate oven 40 minutes or until cooked when tested. Stand few minutes, turn onto wire rack to cool.

BANANA ORANGE CAKE

125g butter
2 teaspoons grated orange rind
½ cup raw sugar
2 eggs
2 ripe bananas
½ cup toasted coconut (see below)
2½ cups wholemeal self-raising flour
½ cup orange juice

Beat butter, orange rind and sugar until creamy. Add eggs one at a time, beating well after each addition; add peeled and finely mashed bananas (you should have ⅔ cup), mix well. Fold in sifted flour and toasted coconut alternately with orange juice. Spread mixture into greased loaf tin with base lined with greaseproof paper (base measures 12cm x 22cm), bake in moderate oven approximately 1 hour. Turn out to cool on wire rack. Serve buttered if desired, or topped with Orange Icing. We used Cream Cheese Frosting (on opposite page) flavored with orange rind.

To toast coconut: Put coconut in heavy pan, stir with wooden spoon over medium heat until coconut is light golden brown, then remove from pan immediately; cool.

SOUR CREAM CARROT CAKE

1 cup wholemeal self-raising flour
1 cup white plain flour
1 teaspoon bicarbonate of soda
2 teaspoons cinnamon
2 teaspoons nutmeg
1 cup brown sugar, lightly packed
1 cup oil (See note for Zucchini Walnut Loaf)
4 eggs
½ cup sour cream
3 cups grated carrot (about 4 carrots)

Sift flours, soda, cinnamon and nutmeg into a large bowl. Add brown sugar and oil; mix well. Put eggs and sour cream into separate bowl; beat

well. Add to flour mixture; mix until smooth. Add grated carrot, mix well. Pour into two greased and lined loaf tins (base measures 9cm x 22cm). Bake in moderately slow oven approximately 45 minutes. Stand few minutes, turn onto wire rack to cool, top with Cream Cheese Frosting.

CREAM CHEESE FROSTING
60g packaged cream cheese
30g butter
1 teaspoon grated lemon rind
1½ cups icing sugar
Mix cream cheese, butter and lemon rind until smooth, gradually beat in sifted icing sugar.

ZUCCHINI WALNUT LOAF

Any salad oil except peanut or olive can be used in this recipe.

3 eggs
1½ cups brown sugar, firmly packed
1 cup oil
125g walnut pieces
1½ cups coarsely grated zucchini (about 3 medium zucchini)
1½ cups wholemeal self-raising flour
1½ cups white plain flour
Combine eggs, sugar and oil in electric mixer or food processor, mix or process until mixture is changed in color; this takes only a short time. Stir in walnuts and zucchini, then sifted flours, return husks from sifter to mixture. Spread mixture into well-greased loaf tin (base measures 12cm x 22cm). Bake in moderate oven approximately 1 hour. Stand few minutes, turn onto wire rack to cool.

PUMPKIN AND PRUNE CAKE

Use ordinary pumpkin (not butternut) for this cake and do not add butter, milk etc when mashing pumpkin.

250g butter
1 teaspoon grated orange rind
1 cup castor sugar
3 eggs
¼ cup orange juice
¾ cup cold mashed pumpkin
½ cup finely chopped prunes
2 cups self-raising flour
⅓ cup milk, approximately
Cream butter, orange rind and sugar together until light and fluffy, add eggs one at a time, beating well after each addition. Stir in orange juice, pumpkin and prunes, then sifted flour alternately with enough milk to give a soft consistency. Spread into greased deep 20cm round cake tin with base lined with greaseproof paper, bake in moderate oven 1 to 1¼ hours, stand 5 minutes, turn onto wire rack to cool.

Clockwise from left: Sour Cream Carrot Cake; Banana Orange Cake; Banana Walnut Cake; Zucchini Walnut Loaf; Pumpkin and Prune Cake.

We've chosen three of our favorite chocolate cakes; they are all moist, but entirely different in taste and texture.

QUICK MIX CHOCOLATE CAKE WITH FUDGE FROSTING

185g butter
¾ cup castor sugar
3 eggs
1 cup self-raising flour
½ cup plain flour
⅓ cup cocoa
½ cup milk
FUDGE FROSTING
60g dark cooking chocolate
15g butter
1½ cups icing sugar
2 tablespoons milk, approximately

Have all ingredients at room temperature. Combine butter, sugar, eggs, sifted dry ingredients and milk in large basin of electric mixer, beat on low speed until ingredients are combined, increase speed to medium, beat for about three minutes or until mixture becomes lighter in color and smoother in texture. Spread mixture evenly into well-greased lamington tin (base measures 16cm x 26cm), bake in moderate oven 30 minutes. Stand few minutes before turning onto wire rack to cool. When cold, top with Fudge Frosting.

Fudge Frosting: Melt chocolate and butter over hot water, stir in sifted icing sugar and enough milk to give thick spreading consistency.

MOIST CHOCOLATE WALNUT CAKE

¾ cup castor sugar
150g butter
4 eggs, separated
125g dark cooking chocolate
125g finely chopped walnuts
½ cup plain flour

Cream butter and sugar until light and fluffy, add egg yolks one at a time, beating well after each addition. Add grated chocolate, sifted flour and walnuts, mix well. Fold in firmly beaten egg whites in two batches, pour mixture into well greased 20cm ring or baba tin. Bake in moderate oven 45 minutes. Stand cake few minutes before turning onto wire rack to cool. If desired, dust top of cold cake with 1 teaspoon each of sifted icing sugar and cocoa.

MOCHA FUDGE CAKE

This cake has a low flour and high sugar content and will develop a sugary crust during the cooking time.

90g dark cooking chocolate
90g butter
1 cup castor sugar
2 eggs
½ cup plain flour
¼ cup self-raising flour
½ cup milk
FILLING AND TOPPING
300ml jar thickened cream
2 teaspoons instant coffee powder
1 tablespoon brandy
1 tablespoon castor sugar
2 tablespoons strawberry jam
2 tablespoons brandy, extra

Melt chocolate over hot water, cool to room temperature. Cream butter and chocolate with sugar, add eggs one at a time, beating well after each addition. Beat in sifted flours and milk. Pour mixture into well-greased deep 20cm round cake tin which has base covered with greased greaseproof paper. Bake in moderately slow oven approximately 1 hour. Stand few minutes before turning onto wire rack to cool. Split cake, fill with jam mixture and some of the cream mixture. Spread top and sides with remaining cream mixture, decorate with strawberries if desired.

Filling and Topping: Dissolve coffee in brandy, add to cream with sugar, beat until firm peaks form. Combine sieved jam with extra brandy. Refrigerate cake at least 30 minutes before cutting.

From top: Mocha Fudge Cake; Moist Chocolate Walnut Cake; Quick-Mix Chocolate Cake with Fudge Frosting.

Homely Cooking

Scones, pikelets and teacakes are easy to make, delicious and always popular. Our homemade muesli is a winner, too.

OVERNIGHT BRAN AND DATE MUFFINS

The muffins can be made and cooked on the same day, but are not as nice as if the mixture is left to stand overnight. Serve piping hot with butter.

1¼ cups plain flour
1 teaspoon bicarbonate of soda
1 teaspoon cinnamon
½ cup sugar
1¾ cups unprocessed bran
125g dates
½ cup oil
1½ cups buttermilk
1 egg

Sift flour with soda, cinnamon and sugar, stir in bran and finely chopped dates. Make well in centre of dry ingredients, add oil, buttermilk and lightly beaten egg, mix only until combined, cover, refrigerate overnight. Next day, drop dessertspoonfuls of mixture into well greased deep muffin tins. Bake in moderately hot oven 20 minutes. Serve hot with butter. Makes 20 muffins.

CRUNCHY HONEY MUESLI

Pepitas are roasted pumpkin seeds; these, and soy bean grits, are available from health food stores.

2 cups rolled oats
1 cup unprocessed bran
1 cup shredded coconut
100g packet pepitas
½ cup skim milk powder
½ cup sesame seeds
½ cup sunflower seed kernels
½ cup soy bean grits
½ cup honey
60g unsalted butter
¼ cup oil

Combine all ingredients in large shallow dish, microwave on full power for 4 minutes, stir the ingredients thoroughly, microwave on full power a further 4 minutes and stir again thoroughly. Microwave a further 4 minutes on full power; cool. Or, bake uncovered in slow oven for 1 hour, stirring every 15 minutes.

Store in airtight container in refrigerator. Add dried fruits or nuts according to taste after cooking.

Makes about 9 cups.

CINNAMON TEACAKE

60g butter
½ cup castor sugar
1 egg
1 teaspoon vanilla
1 cup self-raising flour
⅓ cup milk
15g butter, extra
1 tablespoon castor sugar, extra
1 teaspoon cinnamon

Have butter and egg at room temperature. Cream butter, sugar, egg and vanilla until light and creamy. Stir in sifted flour and milk, beat lightly until smooth. Spread mixture into well-greased 20cm sandwich tin, bake in moderate oven 15 to 20 minutes. Turn onto wire rack, brush top with extra melted butter, sprinkle with combined extra sugar and cinnamon. Serve warm, with butter.

WHOLEMEAL BRAN TEACAKE

60g butter
½ cup brown sugar, firmly packed
1 egg
½ cup wholemeal self-raising flour
½ cup white self-raising flour
½ cup unprocessed bran
½ cup milk
15g butter, extra
1 tablespoon sugar
1 tablespoon coconut
1 teaspoon cinnamon

Cream butter, sugar and egg until light and fluffy. Stir in sifted flours, return husks from sifter to basin, add half the milk, then bran and remaining milk, stir until smooth. Spread mixture into well-greased 20cm sandwich tin, bake in moderate oven 30 minutes. Turn onto wire rack, brush top with extra melted butter, sprinkle with combined sugar, coconut and cinnamon.

Serve warm, with butter.

From left: Crunchy Honey Muesli; Wholemeal Bran Teacake; Cinnamon Turnovers (recipe overleaf); Overnight Bran and Date Muffins; Cinnamon Teacake.

CINNAMON TURNOVERS

This rich scone dough will give you light, flaky turnovers if butter is cold and dough is left slightly lumpy: do not over-handle the dough.

1½ cups self-raising flour
90g butter
⅔ cup milk
60g butter, extra
¼ cup castor sugar
2 teaspoons cinnamon

Sift flour into basin; use coarse grater to grate hard butter over flour. Use knife to toss butter and flour together.

Make well in centre of ingredients, add milk all at once, mix quickly with knife to just combine ingredients. Turn onto a lightly floured surface, knead lightly until dough is smooth.

Roll dough out thinly to about 3mm in thickness, cut into rounds with 10cm cutter. Melt extra butter; combine sugar and cinnamon. Brush one side of each round with melted butter, sprinkle with cinnamon mixture.

Fold round in half with cinnamon side inside, brush on both sides with melted butter, toss in cinnamon mixture. Place on lightly greased oven trays about 2.5cm apart. Repeat with remaining rounds. Bake in hot oven 10 to 15 minutes, or until golden brown. Remove from trays immediately, serve split and buttered.

Makes about 20.

Wholemeal Date Scones (left) are delicious for afternoon tea; Sour Cream and Cheese Scones (right) are delightfully savory.

WHOLEMEAL DATE SCONES

1 cup white self-raising flour
1 cup wholemeal self-raising flour
1 cup unprocessed bran
¼ cup full cream milk powder
60g butter
125g dates
1 cup water, approximately

Sift flours into basin, return husks from sifter to basin, mix in bran and milk powder. Rub in butter, add finely chopped dates. Make well in centre of dry ingredients, stir in enough water to give a soft, sticky dough. Turn dough onto lightly floured surface and knead lightly until smooth. Press dough out to 1cm thickness, cut into rounds with 5cm cutter. Place scones into greased lamington tin (base measures 16cm × 26cm), bake in moderately hot oven 15 to 20 minutes, or until golden brown. Serve hot with butter.

Makes about 15.

SOUR CREAM AND CHEESE SCONES

60g butter
½ cup sour cream
1 egg
125g cheddar cheese
2 cups self-raising flour
pinch cayenne pepper
salt

Melt butter over low heat, add cream and beaten egg, mix well. Stir in finely grated cheese and sifted dry ingredients, mix to soft dough. Turn dough out onto lightly floured surface, knead lightly. Pat out with palm of hand to approximately 2cm thickness, cut into rounds with 5cm cutter. Place close together on lightly greased oven tray. Brush tops with a little milk. Bake in very hot oven 10 to 12 minutes or until golden brown. Serve hot, with butter.

Makes about 12.

WHOLEMEAL PIKELETS
1 cup wholemeal self-raising flour
¼ cup raw sugar
1 egg
⅔ cup milk, approximately
Sift flour into basin, add sugar, make well in centre of dry ingredients, add egg and most of milk, gradually stir dry ingredients into milk mixture; beat until smooth. Add enough of remaining milk to give a smooth, pouring consistency. Mixture will thicken on standing. It may be necessary to add a little more milk to the batter as pikelets are being cooked. Drop tablespoonfuls of mixture onto hot, greased pan; when bubbles appear on top, turn, cook other side.

Makes about 20.

CURRANT AND LEMON PIKELETS
¾ cup self-raising flour
2 tablespoon castor sugar
1 teaspoon grated lemon rind
⅓ cup currants
1 egg
½ cup milk
Sift flour and sugar into basin, add lemon rind and currants; make well in centre of dry ingredients, add combined beaten egg and milk. Gradually stir in flour, mix until smooth. Drop tablespoonfuls of mixture onto hot, greased pan, cook until bubbles appear, turn, cook other side.

Makes about 15.

MIXED FRUIT ROCK CAKES
2 cups self-raising flour
⅓ cup sugar
¼ teaspoon mixed spice
90g butter
1 cup mixed fruit
1 egg
½ cup milk
Sift dry ingredients into bowl, rub in butter. Stir in chopped fruit and combined egg and milk, mix only until all ingredients are moistened. Drop tablespoonfuls of mixture onto lightly greased oven trays. Bake in moderately hot oven 15 to 20 minutes, loosen and cool on trays.

Makes about 15.

APRICOT AND HONEY ROCK CAKES
1 cup wholemeal self-raising flour
1 cup white self-raising flour
¼ cup sugar
¼ teaspoon cinnamon
90g butter
½ cup chopped dried apricots
2 tablespoons sultanas
1 egg
2 tablespoons honey
⅓ cup milk
Sift dry ingredients into basin, rub in butter. Add apricots and sultanas, combine egg and honey, add to mixture with milk, mix only until all ingredients are moistened. Drop tablespoonfuls of mixture in rough heaps onto lightly greased oven trays. Bake in moderately hot oven 15 to 20 minutes, loosen, then cool on trays.

Makes about 15.

From left: Currant and Lemon Pikelets; Wholemeal Pikelets; Mixed Fruit Rock Cakes; Apricot and Honey Rock Cakes.

BISCUITS & SLICES

Here's a variety of biscuits and slices, some homely – ideal for children's lunches and snacks – and some more luscious, perfect to serve with coffee.
The Muesli Apricot Slice is also a delicious – and healthy – addition to children's lunches.

CAMEMBERT TURNOVERS
125g can camembert cheese
125g butter
2 tablespoons finely chopped shallots
2 cups self-raising flour
3 tablespoons milk, approximately
extra milk
125g cheddar cheese
salt, pepper

Have butter and camembert cheese at room temperature. Cream chopped camembert (leave skin on) and butter until light and creamy, stir in shallots, then half the sifted flour, then remaining sifted flour and enough milk to mix to a firm, pliable dough. Turn on to lightly floured surface, knead lightly until smooth, divide dough in half. Roll dough to 3mm thickness, cut into rounds with 8cm cutter, brush with extra milk, place a good pinch of grated cheddar cheese in centre of round, fold in half like a turnover. Place on lightly greased oven trays, press edges together with fork, brush tops with milk, make small cut in top to allow steam to escape, sprinkle with salt and pepper. Bake in moderately hot oven 15 minutes, or until golden brown, remove from trays to cool on wire rack.
Makes about 35.

CHEESE CHIP BISCUITS
60g butter
90g cheese
1 cup lightly crushed packaged potato crisps
½ cup plain flour
pinch dry mustard
pepper

Melt butter in saucepan, add grated cheese, chips, sifted flour, mustard and pepper; mix well. Roll heaped teaspoonfuls of mixture into small balls, flatten with fingers; place on lightly greased oven trays; bake in moderate oven 12 to 15 minutes or until crisp.
Makes about 20.

BACON CRISPS
2 rashers bacon
¾ cup wholemeal plain flour
pinch cayenne
90g butter
90g cheddar cheese
1 tablespoon water, approximately
milk

Remove rind from bacon, chop bacon finely, cook until crisp, drain and cool. Sift flour and cayenne into basin, return husks from sifter to basin, rub in butter, add bacon, add finely grated cheese and just enough water to bind ingredients together. Knead lightly until smooth. Roll out to 3mm thickness, cut into rounds with 5cm cutter, place on lightly greased oven trays. Brush tops lightly with milk, bake in moderate oven 15 minutes, or until golden. Cool on trays.
Makes about 40.

From left: Camembert Turnovers; Cheese Chip Biscuits; Bacon Crisps.

ALMOND BISCUITS

Keep the unbaked dough covered in the refrigerator for up to a fortnight, cut off and bake the biscuits as they are required. Cooked biscuits will keep for up to a month in an airtight container at room temperature. They are not very sweet and are ideal to have with tea or coffee.

125g unblanched almonds
125g butter
½ cup castor sugar
1 egg
2¼ cups plain flour
2 tablespoons water, approximately

Cover almonds with cold water, stand 30 minutes, drain, pat dry on absorbent paper. Cream butter and sugar until light and fluffy, add egg, beat until combined, fold in sifted flour and enough of the 2 tablespoons of water to combine, add almonds; mix well. Divide dough in half; roll each half into a sausage shape, about 3cm thick; wrap in greaseproof paper, refrigerate 1 hour or until firm.

Cut into biscuits 5mm thick. Bake on lightly greased oven trays in moderate oven for 8 to 10 minutes. Cool on wire rack.

Makes about 80.

BRANDIED FRUIT SLICE

1½ cups plain flour
½ cup brown sugar, firmly packed
125g butter
TOPPING
30g butter
2 tablespoons brown sugar
1 tablespoon golden syrup
¼ cup self-raising flour
90g glace cherries
90g sultanas
90g dried apricots
90g slivered almonds
¼ cup brandy

Combine sifted flour and brown sugar in bowl, rub in butter. Press firmly into lightly greased lamington tin (base measures 16cm × 26cm). Spoon fruit Topping evenly over base, bake in moderate oven for 30 minutes. Cool in tin, cut when cold.

Topping: Beat together butter, brown sugar, golden syrup, sifted flour and brandy. Add halved cherries and chopped dried apricots, stir in sultanas and almonds.

CHOC-WALNUT SLICE

1½ cups plain flour
2 tablespoons brown sugar
125g butter
FILLING
2 eggs
1 teaspoon cinnamon
¾ cup brown sugar, lightly packed
½ teaspoon baking powder
125g walnut pieces
CHOCOLATE ICING
125g dark cooking chocolate
1 cup icing sugar
60g butter
1 tablespoon water

Sift flour into bowl, add sugar, rub in butter, mix with hand until ingredients cling together, press dough into greased lamington tin (base measures 16cm × 26cm). Bake in moderate oven 15 minutes. Spread with Filling, bake further 15 minutes in moderate oven. When cold top with Chocolate Icing; cut when set.

Filling: Combine eggs, cinnamon, sugar, baking powder and chopped walnuts in bowl, mix well.

Chocolate Icing: Melt chopped chocolate over hot water, gradually beat in sifted icing sugar, butter and water.

BUTTER OAT SNAPS

1 cup rolled oats
1 cup plain flour
¾ cup coconut
¾ cup raw sugar
125g butter
2 tablespoons honey
2 tablespoons water
1 teaspoon bicarbonate of soda

Combine oats, sifted flour, coconut and sugar in basin, mix in combined melted butter, honey, water and soda. Roll teaspoonfuls of mixture into balls, place about 5cm apart on lightly greased oven trays. Bake in moderate oven 10 to 15 minutes, or until golden brown; cool on trays.

Makes about 30.

SESAME SEED SQUARES

250g (1½ cups) sesame seeds
1½ cups coconut
⅓ cup peanut butter
½ cup honey
½ cup raw sugar
1 teaspoon vanilla

Combine all ingredients thoroughly. Press evenly into lightly greased lamington tin (base measures 16cm × 26cm). Bake in slow oven 30 minutes, or until mixture is light golden brown. Cut into squares while hot, cool in tin.

SOUR CREAM SULTANA BISCUITS

60g butter
2 teaspoons grated lemon rind
1 cup castor sugar
1 egg
1⅓ cups plain flour
½ teaspoon bicarbonate of soda
½ cup sour cream
½ cup sultanas
1 cup coconut

Cream butter and lemon rind, add sugar, beat well; add egg, beat until light and fluffy. Stir in sifted flour and soda with sour cream; mix in sultanas. Roll teaspoonfuls of mixture into balls, roll in coconut, place on lightly greased oven trays about 5cm apart. Bake in moderate oven 10 to 15 minutes until golden brown. Cool on trays.

Makes about 35.

MARBLED CHOCOLATE CHEESECAKE SLICE

185g butter
¼ cup cocoa
1 cup sugar
2 eggs
1 cup plain flour
250g cream cheese
⅓ cup sugar, extra
1 teaspoon vanilla
1 egg, extra

Melt butter with cocoa. Remove from heat, add sugar, whisk in eggs. Stir in sifted flour, beat until smooth. Pour mixture into greased lamington tin (base measures 16cm × 26cm). Beat cheese, extra sugar and vanilla together, add extra egg, pour over chocolate mixture, swirl through with knife for marbled effect. Bake in moderate oven 40 minutes. Cool in tin, cut when cold.

MUESLI APRICOT SLICE

½ cup untoasted muesli
½ cup self-raising flour
¼ cup rolled oats
¼ cup coconut
125g dried apricots
½ cup brown sugar, firmly packed
185g butter
2 tablespoons golden syrup
2 eggs

Mix muesli, sifted flour, oats, coconut, chopped apricots and sugar together in a bowl. Melt butter and golden syrup together over low heat, pour into muesli mixture. Stir in lightly beaten eggs, mix all ingredients well. Pour into well-greased lamington tin (base measures 16cm × 26cm). Bake in moderate oven 30 minutes or until slice shrinks slightly from side of tin. Cool in tin, cut when cold.

Clockwise from top right: Almond Biscuits; Brandied Fruit Slice; Choc-Walnut Slice; Butter Oat Snaps; Sesame Seed Squares; Sour Cream Sultana Biscuits; Marbled Chocolate Cheesecake Slice; Muesli Apricot Slice.

BREAD

Breads are satisfying to make if you have the time. Remember, bread freezes well and it is often just as easy to make several loaves as it is to make one. We have found plastic food wrap to be excellent for covering the basins in which bread is proving. Be sure bread is cooked through; when cooking time has expired, remove bread from tin and tap base of bread firmly with fingers. If it sounds hollow, it is cooked; if not, return to oven, preferably out of the tin (see method for the crisp crusted Wholemeal Bran Bread; this can be applied to any bread). To substitute dry yeast for compressed yeast, note that 30g of compressed yeast equals 3 teaspoons of dry yeast: follow directions on packet for using dried yeast.

FOOD PROCESSOR RYE BREAD

2 teaspoons dry yeast
3 tablespoons sugar
1 cup warm water
3 cups plain flour
½ cup rye flour
1½ teaspoons salt
¼ cup full cream milk powder
2 tablespoons oil
1 egg
3 tablespoons kibbled rye

Place yeast, sugar and warm water in bowl, stir until sugar is dissolved, stand 10 minutes or until frothy. Place flours, salt and milk powder in bowl of processor; process few seconds.

While motor is running, add yeast mixture, process until combined. Add oil and egg, process few seconds; scrape down sides of bowl, process further few seconds. Scrape mixture onto floured surface, knead into a ball. Place in greased bowl, cover with plastic wrap and stand in warm place until doubled in bulk, about 1 hour.

Punch down dough, knead on floured surface into loaf shape. Sprinkle base and sides of well greased loaf tin with 2 tablespoons of the kibbled rye, place dough in tin, stand in warm place uncovered 40 minutes or until doubled in bulk.

Brush top with a little milk, sprinkle with remaining kibbled rye. Bake in moderately hot oven 15 minutes, reduce heat to moderate, bake further 40 minutes. Turn out onto wire rack to cool.

WHITE BREAD VARIATION

2 teaspoons dry yeast
½ cup warm water
2 teaspoons sugar
3 cups plain flour
1½ teaspoons salt
¾ cup warm water, extra

Prepare and bake bread the same as Rye Bread above.

WHITE MILK BREAD

1kg plain flour
½ cup full cream milk powder
2 teaspoons salt
45g compressed yeast
2 cups warm water, approximately
60g butter
1 egg yolk

Sift flour, powdered milk and salt into bowl, rub in butter. Dissolve yeast in half cup of the warm water. Make well in centre of dry ingredients, add yeast mixture and enough of the remaining warm water to mix to a firm dough. Turn onto lightly floured surface, knead until smooth and elastic. Put in bowl, cover, stand in warm place 30 minutes or until doubled in bulk. Punch dough down, turn onto lightly floured surface, knead until smooth. Divide dough in half, knead each half until smooth. Place in two greased loaf tins uncovered. Stand in warm place until dough reaches edge of tin, about 30 minutes. Brush tops with beaten egg yolk, bake in hot oven 15 minutes, reduce heat to moderately hot, bake further 30 minutes.

WHOLEMEAL BRAN BREAD

1kg wholemeal plain flour
1¼ cups plain white flour
1 cup gluten flour
½ cup skim milk powder
2 teaspoons salt
2½ cups unprocessed bran
1 teaspoon sugar
30g compressed yeast
3½ cups warm water, approximately

Sift flours into large basin, return husks from sifter to basin, add milk powder and salt, mix in bran. Make well in centre, add sugar, crumbled yeast and ½ cup of the water; do not mix in any flour. Cover basin with plastic food wrap, stand in warm place for 15 minutes, or until the mixture in the centre has become foamy.

Gradually work in enough of the remaining water to give a firm, pliable dough. Turn onto floured surface, knead well for about 5 minutes, or until dough is smooth and elastic. Place in large greased basin, cover with plastic food wrap, stand in warm place 1 hour or until dough has doubled in bulk.

Turn dough onto floured surface, knead until smooth. Divide in half, knead each half into a loaf shape, place in two greased loaf tins. Stand uncovered in warm place 30 minutes or until dough is well risen. Bake in moderately hot oven 40 minutes.

Remove loaves from tins, place on their sides on oven racks, bake further 10 minutes, turn loaves, bake further 10 minutes, cool on wire rack.

Clockwise from top left: White Milk Bread; Food Processor White Bread; Wholemeal Bran Bread; Food Processor Rye Bread.

Try these recipes and you will be convinced it is not necessary to use yeast to make delicious breads. They will all freeze well; slice before freezing for easier handling.

BRAN BREAD

This is a recipe sent in by a reader some years ago. One slice of this bread provides two tablespoons of bran per day. The bread can be sliced, frozen, and one slice taken out each day; it is delicious toasted.

4 cups self-raising flour
1½ tablespoons baking powder
2 teaspoons salt
2½ cups unprocessed bran
15g butter
2 tablespoons golden syrup or honey
½ cup water
1¼ cups milk, approximately

Sift flour, baking powder and salt into basin, add bran, mix well. Combine butter, golden syrup and water in pan, heat until butter is melted, add milk. Pour liquid into well in centre of dry ingredients, mix with knife to a firm dough. Turn onto floured surface, knead lightly until smooth. Press into well-greased loaf tin, brush top with milk. Cover loosely with piece of greased aluminium foil, pleated lengthwise down the centre to allow room for bread to rise. Bake in moderate oven 1 hour, remove from tin, return to oven on oven tray, bake uncovered further 20 to 30 minutes, cool on wire rack.

BEER BREAD

3¾ cups self-raising flour
2 teaspoons salt
2 teaspoons sugar
375ml can beer

Sift dry ingredients into basin, make well in centre, add beer, use a knife to mix to a soft, sticky dough. Turn onto floured surface, knead lightly until smooth.

Place into well greased loaf tin, brush top with a little milk, bake in moderately hot oven 50 minutes. Turn onto wire rack to cool.

WHOLEMEAL VARIATION

2 cups white self-raising flour
2½ cups wholemeal self-raising flour
¼ cup unprocessed bran

Substitute above ingredients for self-raising flour, then follow Beer Bread recipe.

MILK BREAD

2¾ cups self-raising flour
1 teaspoon salt
1 teaspoon baking powder
60g butter
2 tablespoons wheatgerm
1 tablespoon unprocessed bran
1 teaspoon grated lemon rind
1 egg
1 cup milk, approximately

Sift flour, salt and baking powder into basin. Rub in butter, add wheatgerm, bran and lemon rind; make well in centre, mix in beaten egg and enough milk to mix to a soft dough. Turn dough onto floured surface, knead lightly until smooth. Press into well-greased loaf tin. Brush top with a little milk, bake in moderately hot oven 10 minutes. Reduce heat to moderate, bake further 40 to 50 minutes.

WHOLEMEAL VARIATION

Use 2 cups white self-raising flour and ¾ cup wholemeal self-raising flour. All other ingredients are the same as for Milk Bread.

BUTTERMILK HEALTH BREAD

2 cups buttermilk
¼ cup honey
¼ cup molasses
2 teaspoons bicarbonate of soda
1 teaspoon salt
1½ cups wholemeal plain flour
1 cup white plain flour
½ cup wheatgerm
½ cup sultanas

Combine buttermilk, honey, molasses, soda and salt in bowl. Sift flours together into buttermilk mixture, return husks from sifter to bowl. Add wheatgerm and sultanas; mix well. Pour mixture into well greased loaf tin. Bake in moderate oven 1 hour. Leave in tin 5 minutes before turning onto wire rack to cool.

Clockwise from bottom left: Milk Bread; Bran Bread; Beer Bread; Buttermilk Health Bread. All these recipes are made without yeast.

DESSERTS

Desserts range from homely and hearty to elegant special treats. A lot of them can be made a day or two in advance for added convenience.

CHOCOLATE SPONGE CHEESECAKE

1 packet sponge mix
3 tablespoons cocoa
1 tablespoon coffee liqueur (Tia Maria or Kahlua)
1 tablespoon milk
250g packet cream cheese
⅓ cup sugar
1 egg
3 teaspoons gelatine
2 tablespoons water
3 tablespoons coffee liqueur, extra
300ml jar thickened cream
2 teaspoons cocoa, extra
2 teaspoons icing sugar
60g flaked almonds

Make sponge according to directions on packet, but add sifted cocoa before starting to beat. Pour mixture into greased deep round 20cm cake tin, bake in moderate oven 40 minutes, turn onto wire rack to cool. When cake is cold, cut two very thin slices from base of cake; slices need to be about 5mm in thickness. Remaining cake can be frozen for future use. Use base of deep round 18cm cake tin as a guide and trim both layers of cake to this size. Line base and side of this 18cm tin with strips of aluminium foil, bringing foil over sides of tin to make cake easy to remove. Place one layer of cake into tin, brush with half the combined Tia Maria and milk.

Have cream cheese at room temperature. Combine in small basin of electric mixer with sugar and egg, beat until smooth. Sprinkle gelatine over water, dissolve over hot water, add extra Tia Maria to gelatine mixture, add to cream cheese mixture, beat in cream until just combined. Pour cream cheese mixture over cake, place remaining layer of cake on top, brush with remaining Tia Maria and milk mixture, refrigerate several hours or overnight until set. Remove from tin, place on serving plate. Dust top with combined sifted extra cocoa and icing sugar, press toasted almonds around side.

To toast almonds: Place almonds on oven tray, bake in moderate oven 5 minutes or until golden brown, cool before using.

RUM CREAM FLAN

Best made the day before serving.

185g (1¼ cups) ground hazelnuts
¼ cup castor sugar
1 egg white
FILLING
125g dark cooking chocolate
300ml jar thickened cream
1 tablespoon rum
2 teaspoons sugar

Combine hazelnuts, sugar and unbeaten egg white; mix well. Roll mixture out between two sheets of greaseproof paper large enough to cover base and side of 20cm flan tin; remove top paper. Press mixture into greased tin; remove other paper. Refrigerate 30 minutes. Lightly press sheet of aluminium foil over hazelnut case to cover completely, bake in moderately slow oven 20 minutes. Remove foil, return case to oven, bake further 5 minutes, cool. Spoon Filling into case. Decorate with extra chocolate. Refrigerate several hours.

Filling: Melt chocolate and half the cream in pan, cool to room temperature. Beat chocolate cream on electric mixer until soft peaks form. Beat remaining cream, rum and sugar until soft peaks form. Swirl chocolate cream into rum cream.

CHOCOLATE MINT FLAN

185g plain chocolate biscuits
125g unsalted butter
FILLING
125g unsalted butter
1 cup icing sugar
100g block peppermint chocolate
1 tablespoon water
2 eggs
TOPPING
30g dark cooking chocolate
½ cup thickened cream

Melt butter in pan, add finely crushed biscuits and mix well. Press crumb mixture over base of 23cm flan tin. Refrigerate 30 minutes. Spoon Filling onto chocolate base, smooth top with knife. Decorate with Topping. Refrigerate several hours before serving.

Filling: Cream butter and sifted icing sugar until light and fluffy. Melt chocolate and water over hot water, cool to room temperature, do not allow to set. Add chocolate to butter mixture, beat on high speed until smooth. Add eggs one at a time, beating well after each addition.

Topping: Grate chocolate, sprinkle over Filling, decorate with whipped cream.

From left: Chocolate Mint Flan; Chocolate Sponge Cheesecake; Rum Cream Flan.

MOIST CHOCOLATE DESSERT CAKE

This cake is best made and served on the same day. Serve warm or cold.

90g dark cooking chocolate
90g unsalted butter
¼ cup water
3 eggs, separated
1 teaspoon vanilla
⅔ cup castor sugar
¼ cup plain flour

Melt chocolate, butter and water in pan. Place mixture into small bowl of electric mixer; beat on medium speed, beat in egg yolks one at a time. Add vanilla, sugar and flour, beat further 3 minutes. Beat egg whites until firm peaks form, gently fold chocolate mixture into egg whites. Pour mixture into 23cm savarin or 20cm ring tin. Place tin in baking dish with hot water to come halfway up side of tin, bake in moderate oven 40 minutes or until top feels firm to touch. Remove from water, cool 5 minutes. Turn onto serving plate, cool to room temperature, sprinkle with icing sugar, serve with whipped cream.

PECAN CREAM PIE

1½ cups plain flour
¼ cup castor sugar
125g butter
1 egg yolk
1 tablespoon cold water, approximately
2 teaspoons castor sugar, extra
FILLING
250g pecans
300ml jar thickened cream
2 tablespoons honey

Sift flour into basin, add sugar, rub in butter, add egg yolk and enough of the water to mix to a firm dough. Refrigerate 30 minutes. Roll half the pastry to fit base and side of 23cm flan tin, add Filling, cover with remaining rolled-out pastry, trim edges. Brush with water, sprinkle lightly with extra castor sugar, put on oven slide; cook in moderately hot oven 10 minutes, reduce heat to moderate, bake further 20 minutes or until golden brown. Serve warm with cream.
Filling: Combine all ingredients.

COFFEE PISTACHIO ROLL

This cake is at its best cooked on the day it is required. There is no liquid in the sponge cake recipe.

3 eggs
½ cup castor sugar
¼ cup cornflour
¼ cup plain flour
¼ cup self-raising flour
COFFEE FILLING
1 tablespoon instant coffee powder
1 tablespoon hot water
3 teaspoons gelatine
1 tablespoon Tia Maria
1 egg
½ cup icing sugar
¾ cup thickened cream
TOPPING
300ml jar thickened cream
3 teaspoons instant coffee powder
3 teaspoons hot water
60g pistachio nuts

Beat eggs and sugar on electric mixer until thick and creamy (up to 10 minutes). Sift dry ingredients over egg mixture and fold through lightly. Spread mixture into greased and paper-lined swiss roll tin (base measures 25cm by 30cm). Bake in moderate oven 15 minutes. Turn onto wire rack covered with greaseproof paper, remove lining paper and roll up loosely from long side. Stand 3 minutes, then unroll, cool to room temperature. Spread Filling over cake, roll up from long side. Place on serving plate. Spread half the Topping over cake, decorate with remaining Topping and chopped pistachio nuts.

To shell pistachio nuts: Drop into pan of boiling water, boil 4 minutes, drain. Shell nuts, peel away skin.
Coffee Filling: Dissolve coffee in water. Combine gelatine and Tia Maria, dissolve over hot water. Beat egg and icing sugar on electric mixer until thick and creamy. Beat in gelatine and coffee mixtures. Beat cream until firm peaks form, gently fold into egg mixture, refrigerate 30 minutes.
Topping: Dissolve coffee in water, cool. Beat cream until firm peaks form, fold in coffee mixture.

FRUIT MINCE CRESCENT

1 Granny Smith apple
185g dried apricots
⅔ cup bottled fruit mince
¼ cup water
1½ cups plain flour
185g butter
⅓ cup ice cold water
egg white
sugar

Place water, peeled and chopped apple and chopped apricots in small pan. Bring slowly to boil, simmer covered 5 minutes. Add fruit mince, mix well, cool.

Sift flour into bowl, coarsely grate cold butter over flour, mix through lightly with fingertips — butter should stay in small lumps evenly throughout pastry. Add iced water, press ingredients together quickly and lightly with hand. Refrigerate 30 minutes. Roll dough out on lightly floured surface to approximately 28cm x 38cm. Spread fruit mince mixture evenly over pastry. Roll up as for swiss roll, starting from the short end. Without cutting through completely, divide into 12 even slices. Place on ungreased oven tray, shape into crescent. Brush wth a little egg white, sprinkle with sugar. Bake in hot oven 30 minutes until golden brown.

APPLE AND PASSIONFRUIT SHORTCAKE

125g butter
½ cup sugar
1 egg
¾ cup self-raising flour
¾ cup plain flour
425g can dessert apple
1 passionfruit
1 teaspoon grated lemon rind
extra sugar

Cream butter and sugar, add egg, beat well. Stir in sifted flours in two batches. Turn onto lightly floured surface, knead lightly until smooth, divide in half, refrigerate 30 minutes. Roll each piece into a 20cm round between 2 sheets of plastic food wrap or greaseproof paper.

Grease and line the base and sides of a 20cm sandwich tin with greaseproof paper. Press one circle of dough into the tin.

Combine apple, passionfruit pulp and lemon rind. Spread over dough, leaving a small border around edge. Sprinkle with 1 tablespoon of extra sugar. Place second round of dough over apple mixture, press edges together.

Brush with water, sprinkle lightly with extra sugar. Bake in moderate oven 35 to 40 minutes. Stand 15 minutes before removing from tin.

Serve warm or cold.

Clockwise from left: Coffee Pistachio Roll; Moist Chocolate Dessert Cake; Pecan Cream Pie; Fruit Mince Crescent.

APPLE PIE

1½ cups plain flour
¾ cup self-raising flour
⅓ cup cornflour
⅓ cup custard powder
185g butter
1 tablespoon sugar
1 egg yolk
⅓ cup water, approximately
1 egg white
extra sugar
FILLING
7 large Granny Smith apples
½ cup water
3 tablespoons sugar
½ teaspoon cinnamon
1 teaspoon grated lemon rind
2 tablespoons apricot jam

Sift flours and custard powder into bowl, rub in butter; add sugar. Make well in centre, add egg yolk and enough water to mix to a firm dough, knead lightly. Cover, refrigerate 1 hour. Roll out just over half pastry on lightly floured surface large enough to line a pie plate (base measures 23cm). Spread base of pastry with apricot jam, top with cold apple mixture.

Roll out remaining pastry; brush edges of pie with lightly beaten egg white, cover with pastry. Press edges together firmly, trim and decorate. Brush top with egg white; sprinkle with extra sugar. Cut a few slits in top of pie to allow steam to escape. Bake in moderately hot oven 20 to 30 minutes or until pie is golden brown.

Filling: Peel, quarter and core apples; cut each quarter in half lengthwise. Put in pan with water, sugar, cinnamon and lemon rind. Cook covered about 5 minutes or until apples are almost tender but still holding their shape. Remove from heat, drain, cool to room temperature.

Clockwise from left: Apple and Passionfruit Shortcake; Apple Pie; Spiced Pumpkin Pie; Coconut Apricot Flan.

SPICED PUMPKIN PIE

You will need about 2 kg dry pumpkin; boil or steam in usual way and mash well with fork when tender. Butternut pumpkin is not suitable.

2 cups plain flour
1 tablespoon icing sugar
185g butter
1 egg yolk
2 tablespoons water, approximately
FILLING
2 cups mashed pumpkin
½ cup brown sugar, firmly packed
1 tablespoon treacle or golden syrup
2 teaspoons mixed spice
2 teaspoons cinnamon
⅔ cup sultanas
⅓ cup currants
⅓ cup mixed peel

Sift dry ingredients into basin, rub in butter, add egg yolk and enough water to mix to a firm, pliable dough. Wrap in plastic food wrap, refrigerate 30 minutes. Roll two thirds of pastry to line base and sides of pie plate (base measures 18cm), spread with Filling, top with remaining pastry; trim and decorate edge. Bake in moderately hot oven 10 minutes, reduce heat to moderate, bake further 20 to 30 minutes or until golden brown. Cool to room temperature before serving. Serve with cream.

Filling: Combine pumpkin with sugar, treacle, spices and fruits, mix well.

COCONUT APRICOT FLAN

1 sheet of ready rolled puff pastry
½ cup apricot jam
2 eggs
½ cup sugar
2 cups coconut
15g butter

Thaw pastry to room temperature, place in 20cm flan tin, trim the pastry around top of tin with sharp knife. Brush base of pastry with half the sieved jam. Beat eggs until thick, add sugar, beat until thick and creamy, stir in coconut and melted butter. Spread evenly over jam, bake in moderate oven 30 minutes or until golden brown. Brush with remaining sieved jam while still hot. Serve warm with whipped cream.

FROZEN APRICOT CREAM

250g glace apricots
125g glace ginger
125g toasted slivered almonds
¼ cup brandy
2 eggs
½ cup icing sugar
3 x 300ml jars thickened cream

Chop apricots and ginger about the same size as the almonds, combine with brandy. Beat eggs until thick and creamy, add sifted sugar, beat until thick. Beat cream until thick. Combine fruit mixture, almonds and egg mixture, fold into cream. Spread evenly into basin or mould of 6 cup capacity, cover with aluminium foil, freeze overnight. To serve, dip basin into hot water for a second or two, turn pudding on to serving plate, refrigerate for 30 minutes then stand at room temperature for up to further 30 minutes (depending on weather) before cutting.

Serves 8.

Note: Spread almonds on flat tray, bake in moderate oven 5 to 10 minutes or until lightly browned, cool. It is important the cream used in this recipe be beaten as thickly as possible so it will be firm enough to suspend the fruit.

Clockwise from left: Raspberry Freezer Cake; Frozen Apricot Cream; Groggy Grapes with Berry Sauce; Grand Marnier Pots de Creme.

GROGGY GRAPES WITH BERRY SAUCE

Grapes marinated in Grand Marnier syrup can be prepared the day before. Make the Berry Sauce a day or two before. We used raspberries for the brightest color but any berry, fresh or frozen, can be used.

500g white seedless grapes
½ cup sugar
2 tablespoons water
1 tablespoon Grand Marnier
vanilla icecream
BERRY SAUCE
250g frozen raspberries
2 tablespoons icing sugar
1 tablespoon Grand Marnier

Remove stems from grapes, peel grapes, place in basin. Add sugar to water in pan, stir over heat until sugar is dissolved, bring to boil, remove from heat, add Grand Marnier, pour over grapes. Cover, refrigerate several hours or overnight. Divide between four glasses, top with ice cream and warm Berry Sauce just before serving.

Berry Sauce: Thaw berries, blend or process with sugar until smooth, push through sieve, discard seeds, add Grand Marnier. Warm before serving.

Serves 4.

GRAND MARNIER POTS de CREME

½ cup sugar
300ml jar thickened cream
¼ cup milk
2 teaspoons grated orange rind
4 egg yolks
2 tablespoons Grand Marnier
GLAZED ORANGE STRIPS
1 orange
¾ cup water
½ cup sugar

Heat sugar, cream and milk in pan until just below boiling point, add orange rind. Whisk cream mixture into egg yolks with Grand Marnier. Pour into four small heatproof dishes, stand in baking dish with hot water to come halfway up sides of dishes. Cover loosely with aluminium foil, bake in moderate oven 40 to 45 minutes. Remove from water, cool, refrigerate. Serve topped with whipped cream and Glazed Orange Strips.

Glazed Orange Strips: Peel rind from orange with vegetable peeler. Bring water to boil, add rind, boil 5 minutes; drain. Cut into thin strips. Place water and sugar in pan, stir over heat until sugar is dissolved, bring to boil, add rind and cook until transparent (approximately 4 minutes). Remove rind from pan, place on foil to cool.

Serves 4.

RASPBERRY FREEZER CAKE

This freezer cake can be made up to 3 months in advance. It cuts superbly and the flavor is fresh and summery.

150g unsalted butter
¾ cup castor sugar
4 eggs, separated
1 cup plain flour
½ cup self raising flour
RASPBERRY SYRUP
450g can raspberries
2 tablespoons icing sugar
2 tablespoons kirsch
BUTTER CREAM
185g unsalted butter
⅓ cup icing sugar
2 tablespoons kirsch
½ × 210g roll packaged marzipan

Cream soft butter and ½ cup sugar for 5 minutes or until light and creamy. Add egg yolks one at a time, beating well after each addition. Beat egg whites to soft peaks, add remaining ¼ cup sugar gradually, beat until dissolved. Fold sifted flours into creamed butter mixture, then fold in egg white mixture in two batches. Spread into well greased loaf tin (base measures 12 cm x 22 cm), bake in moderate oven 35 to 40 minutes. Turn onto rack to cool. When cold, split into three even layers. Place bottom layer on oven tray, brush with a third of the Raspberry Syrup (pierce cake with skewer to allow syrup to soak into cake).

Spread with a third of the Butter Cream, top with half the reserved mashed raspberries. Top with another layer of cake. Brush with another third of Raspberry Syrup. Cover with another third of the Butter Cream, then rolled marzipan; spread thin layer of Butter Cream over marzipan.

Brush cut side of last layer of cake with remaining syrup, place crust side up on top of marzipan layer. Push down on the cake with a board or other firm object to flatten slightly, spread remaining Butter Cream on top of cake. Cover carefully with aluminium foil, freeze overnight or until required.

To serve: Trim sides of cake and slice while still frozen. Cake will thaw enough to serve in about 5 minutes.

Raspberry Syrup: Drain raspberries, reserve. Measure syrup, reserve half for Butter Cream. To remaining half of syrup add icing sugar and kirsch, stir to dissolve.

Butter Cream: Cream soft butter with electric mixer for five minutes. Push half the reserved raspberries and remaining syrup through sieve, discard seeds. Gradually add raspberry mixture to butter while creaming. Gradually beat in sifted icing sugar and kirsch. Roll marzipan between 2 sheets of plastic food wrap to the same size as a cake layer.

WALNUT AND APRICOT MERINGUE TORTE

The meringue layers can be cooked about a week in advance and stored in an airtight container. Assemble the cake up to 6 hours before serving.

4 egg whites
1 cup castor sugar
150g walnuts
80g dried apricots
1 tablespoon brandy
300ml jar thickened cream
350g can apricots
PRALINE
½ cup castor sugar
2 tablespoons water
½ cup chopped walnuts

Chop walnuts roughly, place on oven tray, bake in moderately slow oven 5 minutes, cool. Beat egg whites until soft peaks form, add sugar gradually, beat until dissolved, fold in walnuts. Grease two large oven trays, dust lightly with cornflour, mark a 25cm circle on each one; divide meringue mixture between the trays. Bake in moderately slow oven 1 hour, change positions of trays after half the cooking time, cool.

Cover dried apricots with boiling water, stand covered 20 to 30 minutes, drain, puree in blender or processor, push through sieve. Stir in brandy, fold in whipped cream.

Place one meringue layer on serving plate, spread with one third of the apricot cream, top with remaining layer, spread and decorate with remaining apricot cream. Decorate with Praline and drained canned apricots.

Praline: Place sugar and water in small pan, stir without boiling until sugar has dissolved, boil rapidly 5 to 10 minutes or until a light golden colour, add walnuts, pour mixture onto lightly greased oven tray; when set, break into pieces and chop finely.

Walnut and Apricot Meringue Torte (back); Strawberry Cream Meringues.

STRAWBERRY CREAM MERINGUES

These meringues may be stored in an airtight container for up to a week before required.

3 egg whites
¾ cup castor sugar
300ml jar thickened cream
1 punnet strawberries
2 teaspoons sugar, extra
2 teaspoons Grand Marnier
1 tablespoon icing sugar
1 tablespoon Grand Marnier, extra

Cover a large oven tray with aluminium foil; using a scone cutter as a guide, mark out eight 6cm circles on the foil.

To make meringues: beat egg whites until soft peaks form. Gradually beat in sugar a tablespoon at a time. Make sure each tablespoonful of sugar is dissolved before adding any more. Spoon meringue into a large piping bag fitted with a plain piping tube approximately 2cm in diameter. Pipe mixture over circles marked on foil so they are about 2cm thick.

Bake in very slow oven about 1 hour or until dry to touch. Allow meringues to cool in oven with door ajar.

When cool, carefully remove from foil. Wash and hull strawberries, mash about one third of them. Beat cream and extra sugar until firm peaks form, fold in Grand Marnier and the mashed strawberries.

Spoon or pipe strawberry cream on to flat side of one meringue, sandwich together with a second meringue, place on serving dish. Puree remaining strawberries in processor or blender with icing sugar and extra Grand Marnier. Pour strawberry puree over meringues.

Serves 4.

ICECREAMS & SORBETS

We've chosen 5 deliciously different icecreams, all glamorous enough to serve at dinner parties. Remember to keep them covered while freezing to help prevent crystals forming. Sorbets are wonderfully refreshing and light; make them up to a week before required and keep them covered while in the freezer.

TWO-BERRY ICECREAM

250g frozen or fresh raspberries
250g frozen or fresh strawberries
4 egg yolks
1 cup sugar
2 X 300ml jars thickened cream
1 tablespoon lemon juice
1 tablespoon Grand Marnier

Thaw berries to room temperature. Push raspberries through sieve; discard seeds. Beat half the egg yolks and half the sugar in small basin of electric mixer until thick and creamy. Heat half the cream in pan to just below boiling point, add egg yolk mixture to pan, whisk over low heat until thickened. Do not boil. Remove from heat, cool slightly, add raspberry puree. Pour mixture into 1 litre mould, cover with aluminium foil, freeze.

Push strawberries through sieve; discard seeds. Beat remaining egg yolks and sugar until thick and creamy, as above. Heat remaining cream in pan to just below boiling point, add yolk mixture to pan, whisk over low heat until thickened. Do not boil. Remove from heat, cool few minutes, stir in lemon juice, Grand Marnier and strawberry puree. Pour mixture over frozen raspberry mixture, cover with foil, freeze. Turn on to plate, decorate with strawberries if desired.

Serves 6 to 8.

CHESTNUT AND CHOCOLATE ICECREAM

CHESTNUT ICECREAM
3 eggs
1 tablespoon sugar
250g can chestnut spread
1 tablespoon Grand Marnier
300ml container thickened cream
CHOCOLATE ICECREAM
185g dark cooking chocolate
2 eggs
2 tablespoons sugar
300ml jar thickened cream
RASPBERRY SAUCE
375g frozen or fresh raspberries
¼ cup sugar
1 tablespoon Grand Marnier

Chestnut Icecream: Beat eggs and sugar in small bowl of electric mixer until thick and creamy, about 5 minutes. Add chestnut spread, beat until well combined, stir in Grand Marnier. Whip cream until soft peaks form, fold into chestnut mixture. Pour mixture into cake tin and freeze. When frozen, break up mixture with fork, place in bowl of electric mixer and beat until smooth. Line base and sides of loaf tin with aluminium foil to come 5cm over edge of tin. Pour half the Chestnut Icecream over base of tin, freeze. Return remaining icecream to cake tin, freeze. When chestnut layer in the loaf tin is firm, pour half the Chocolate Icecream on top of the chestnut layer and freeze. Repeat layers and freeze. Serve with Raspberry Sauce.

Chocolate Icecream: Melt chocolate over hot water; cool. Beat eggs and sugar until thick and creamy, add chocolate and beat until combined. Whip cream until soft peaks form, fold into chocolate mixture. Pour mixture into cake tin and freeze. When frozen, break up mixture with fork and beat on mixer until smooth.

Raspberry Sauce: Thaw berries. Combine with sugar and Grand Marnier. Push mixture through sieve, discard seeds. Refrigerate Sauce until required.

Serves 4 to 6.

Chestnut and Chocolate Icecream (left) and Two-Berry Icecream (right) are both elegant desserts for a special dinner party.

APRICOT ICECREAM

250g dried apricots
5cm strip lemon rind
1 tablespoon lemon juice
2 x 300ml jars thickened cream
4 egg yolks
⅔ cup castor sugar
2 tablespoons Grand Marnier

Place apricots and lemon rind in pan, cover with cold water, bring to boil, reduce heat, simmer covered 15 minutes or until tender; drain, discard lemon rind. Puree apricots in food processor or push through sieve; add lemon juice and Grand Marnier.

Combine egg yolks and sugar in bowl, beat until thick. Warm cream in pan, whisk in egg mixture; whisk constantly over heat until slightly thickened; do not boil. Remove from heat, fold in apricot puree. Pour mixture into loaf tin, cover with aluminium foil, freeze; when partly frozen, beat well on mixer, then refreeze.

Serves 6.

COFFEE CARAMEL ICECREAM

Caramel does not set hard, but forms a firm sauce when the icecream is served.

2-litre carton vanilla icecream
⅓ cup evaporated milk
¾ cup sugar
12 packaged white marshmallows
2 teaspoons instant coffee powder
1 teaspoon vanilla
1 tablespoon Tia Maria or Kahlua
60g walnuts

Combine milk and sugar in pan, stir over heat until sugar is dissolved, bring to boil, reduce heat slightly, boil as fast as possible, without boiling mixture over, for 5 minutes. Remove from heat, allow bubbles to subside. Add marshmallows and coffee, stir until marshmallows are melted, add vanilla and Tia Maria, refrigerate until cold, stir in coarsely chopped walnuts.

Place icecream in large basin, stir with wooden spoon until just softened, quickly fold coffee mixture through to give marbled effect. Spread into loaf tin, cover with aluminium foil, freeze several hours or overnight before serving.

Serves 8.

MINTED ICECREAM

⅓ cup sugar
½ cup water
1 cup mint leaves, firmly packed
1 tablespoon lemon juice
2 egg yolks
¼ cup sugar, extra
300ml jar thickened cream

Place sugar and water in pan, stir over low heat until sugar is dissolved. Bring to boil, boil rapidly 1 minute. Remove from heat, add chopped mint leaves, stand 20 minutes. Strain leaves, pressing firmly to extract juices; discard leaves. Add lemon juice to syrup, mix well. Combine egg yolks and extra sugar in pan, stir over low heat until slightly thickened; do not boil; cool. Beat cream until soft peaks form, gently fold in cold egg yolk mixture and syrup. Pour into mould or loaf tin, cover with aluminium foil, freeze overnight or until set.

Serves 6.

LEMON SORBET
½ cup sugar
½ cup water
½ cup white wine
½ cup lemon juice
1 egg white
Combine sugar, water and wine in small pan, stir over heat until sugar is dissolved; bring to boil, reduce heat, simmer uncovered 10 minutes; cool. Combine lemon juice and sugar syrup; pour into shallow tray, freeze until firm.

Place mixture in chilled bowl, beat until smooth with wooden spoon. Fold in stiffly beaten egg white, return to tray, freeze until firm.

Serves 4.

STRAWBERRY SORBET
3 tablespoons gin
1 punnet strawberries
½ cup sugar
1½ cups water
½ cup dry white wine
2 tablespoons lemon juice
1 egg white
Halve strawberries, place in bowl with gin, cover, refrigerate several hours or overnight.

Place sugar and water in pan, stir over heat until sugar has dissolved. Bring mixture to boil, boil gently, uncovered, 10 minutes (there should be about ¾ cup syrup left); cool. Puree strawberries and gin in blender or food processor, add to wine, lemon juice and cold sugar syrup; mix well.

Pour mixture into freezer tray, freeze until almost set. Remove from freezer, break up with fork, fold in beaten egg white, blend well. Return mixture to freezer, freeze until set, stirring occasionally with a fork.

Serves 4.

EASY ORANGE SORBET
170ml can frozen unsweetened orange juice concentrate
2 tablespoons lemon juice
1 cup water
1 tablespoon sugar
1 egg white
Combine water, sugar and lemon juice in pan, stir over low heat until sugar is dissolved, bring to boil, reduce heat, simmer 2 minutes, add orange juice concentrate; pour into freezer tray, freeze until just beginning to set.

Mix with a fork until mushy, fold in stiffly beaten egg white. Return to freezer until frozen.

Serves 4.

CHRISTMAS PUDDINGS

Christmas brings many calls for pudding recipes; these 3 are popular. Choose the method that suits you best; each recipe serves at least 8 people.

BOILED CHRISTMAS PUDDING
250g raisins
250g sultanas
185g currants
185g mixed peel
1 teaspoon grated lemon rind
2 tablespoons lemon juice
2 tablespoons brandy
250g butter
2 cups brown sugar, firmly packed
5 large eggs
1¼ cups plain flour
½ teaspoon nutmeg
½ teaspoon mixed spice
250g (5½ cups) day-old white breadcrumbs, loosely packed

Chop raisins, combine in large basin with sultanas, currants, peel, lemon rind, lemon juice and brandy, mix well. Cover, stand overnight. Beat butter and sugar in large basin of electric mixer until combined. Beat in eggs one at a time. Add creamed mixture to fruit mixture with sifted dry ingredients and breadcrumbs; mix well.

To Boil: Boil 6 hours and further 1½ hours on day of serving. Dip prepared pudding cloth into boiling water; use rubber gloves to protect hands, wring excess water from cloth. Have ⅓ cup plain flour close to cloth. Spread hot cloth out on bench, quickly rub flour into cloth to cover an area about 38cm in diameter, leave flour thicker in the centre of the cloth, where the skin will need to be thickest.

Place cloth in colander or basin, place mixture in centre. Gather ends of cloth together, hold pudding up, pat into shape with hand.

Tie pudding securely with string, as close to pudding mixture as possible; tie loop in string to make pudding easier to lift. Pull ends of cloth tightly to make sure pudding is as round as possible. Have ready a large boiler three-quarters full of rapidly boiling water. Gently but quickly lower pudding into water, quickly replace lid, boil rapidly for specified cooking time. Replenish boiler with boiling water as it evaporates; there must be enough water for the pudding to move freely and the water should be deep enough for the pudding to float at all times.

After required cooking time, use handle of wooden spoon to lift pudding from water; place handle through looped string. Lift carefully but quickly from water; do not put pudding down as it is too soft at this stage. Suspend pudding from drawer or cupboard handle.

It is important the pudding can swing freely without touching anything. Twist ends of cloth around supporting string to keep wet ends away from pudding. If pudding has been cooked correctly, the cloth will begin to dry out in patches within a few minutes. Leave pudding to dry overnight. Next day, when pudding is cold, remove from handle, cut string, loosen cloth away from top of pudding, scrape away any excess flour, leave at room temperature for a day or two (time will depend on humidity of the weather) or until the cloth is completely dry around the top of the pudding. Tie pudding cloth again with string, place pudding in airtight plastic bag, refrigerate until required.

To serve pudding hot: Remove pudding from refrigerator about 12 hours before it is to be reheated. Prepare for reheating the pudding about 3 hours before it is to be served.

Have large boiler three-quarters full of boiling water, gently lower pudding into boiler, boil for specified time. Suspend hot pudding for 10 minutes, tuck ends of cloth into string away from top of pudding.

Have serving plate and scissors ready. Place pudding on bench, near to plate, cut string quickly, gently ease cloth away from pudding until about a quarter of the pudding is uncovered. Using a towel to protect hands, gently invert on to serving plate, slowly and gently pull cloth away.

Leave pudding further 20 minutes at least before cutting. The longer the pudding is left standing, the darker the 'skin' will become.

To serve pudding cold: Reheat pudding the day before it is to be served. Proceed as above, then leave pudding to become completely cold, this will take at least 12 hours; cover with plastic food wrap, refrigerate.

Pudding cloth: Buy half a metre of unbleached calico 122cm wide; cut in half, trim to give two square cloths. Soak calico in cold water overnight. Next day, boil for 20 minutes, then rinse well. Cloth is now ready for use. After pudding has been reheated and removed from cloth, soak cloth in cold water, boil and rinse well.

STEAMED CHRISTMAS PUDDING
500g mixed fruit
125g dates
125g raisins
1 cup water
½ cup white sugar
½ cup brown sugar, lightly packed
125g butter
1 teaspoon bicarbonate of soda
2 eggs
1 cup plain flour
1 cup self-raising flour
1 teaspoon mixed spice
½ teaspoon cinnamon
2 tablespoons rum

Combine chopped fruits, water, sugars and butter. Stir until butter has melted, bring to boil; reduce heat, simmer uncovered 8 minutes, stir in soda. Stand until mixture has become cold. Stir in eggs, sifted dry ingredients and rum.

Steam in well-greased 10 cup steamer for 5 hours, steam further 1½ hours on day of serving.

To Steam: Fill pudding mixture into well-greased aluminium steamer, cover with large piece of aluminium foil. Put lid firmly on steamer, then crush surplus foil firmly around the lid to help form a good seal. Put pudding in large boiler with enough boiling water to come halfway up side of steamer. Cover with tight-fitting lid, replenish with more boiling water as necessary during cooking time.

When cold, store in steamer in refrigerator for up to 6 weeks.

EASY PLUM PUDDING
1kg mixed fruit
3 eggs
1 cup brown sugar, firmly packed
300ml carton cream
2¼ cups plain flour
1 teaspoon nutmeg
1 teaspoon bicarbonate of soda

Chop fruit, place in large basin. Beat eggs and sifted brown sugar until thick and creamy, add to fruit with cream; mix well. Add sifted dry ingredients; mix well.

Boil or steam 5 hours; boil or steam further 1½ hours on day of serving to reheat. If steaming, place mixture into well-greased 10 cup steamer.

From top: Boiled Christmas Pudding; Easy Plum Pudding; Steamed Christmas Pudding.

SWEET TREATS

Except for the Toffee Dipped Grapes, these Sweet Treats can be made at least a day before required. Store them in the refrigerator if the weather is warm.

WHITE CHOCOLATE TRUFFLES

We have used Amaretto for these truffles because of its almond flavor. Grand Marnier, Curacao or Cointreau would be ideal substitutes and will give a citrus flavor to the truffles.

30g dried apricots
1 tablespoon Amaretto liqueur
125g white chocolate
½ cup blanched almonds
75g dark cooking chocolate
15g Copha
100g chocolate sprinkles

Finely chop dried apricots, soak in Amaretto for at least 10 minutes. Melt white chocolate over hot water, stir in finely chopped almonds and apricot Amaretto mixture. Refrigerate until firm. Roll into 1.5cm balls, refrigerate. Melt dark chocolate and Copha over hot water. Dip truffles in chocolate, roll in chocolate sprinkles. Set and store in refrigerator.

Makes approximately 30.

ALMOND SPLINTERS

150g slivered almonds
250g dark cooking chocolate

Spread almonds on flat oven tray, bake in moderate oven 5 to 10 minutes or until golden brown, cool. Melt chocolate over hot water, add almonds, mix well. Drop teaspoons of mixture into foil patty cases, stand in cool place or refrigerate until set. Store in refrigerator in warm weather.

Makes about 30.

CHOCOLATE PUDDINGLETS

Use leftover boiled Christmas pudding to make these (steamed pudding is too cakey in texture to form balls). Use a melon baller 2.5cm in diameter to make the balls, roll between hands to make as smooth as possible. Melt chocolate over hot water (250g chocolate is sufficient to coat 24 pudding balls), dip balls in chocolate, stand on aluminium foil-covered tray, refrigerate until set. Place balls in paper or foil cases. Keep refrigerated.

When chocolate is firm a favorite liqueur can be injected into the puddinglets with a syringe (available from most hardware and specialty kitchenware shops).

Clockwise from bottom right: Chocolate Puddinglets; Sesame Nut Caramels; Chocolate Collettes; White Chocolate Truffles; Almond Splinters.

CHOCOLATE COLLETTES

125g dark cooking chocolate
30g pistachio nuts
FILLING
90g dark cooking chocolate
2 tablespoons cream
15g butter
1 egg yolk
2 teaspoons rum

Melt chocolate over hot water; cool. Spread inside of small foil cases with chocolate using brush or back of teaspoon, refrigerate until set. Pipe Filling into cases, sprinkle with slivered pistachio nuts. Refrigerate 15 minutes, peel away foil cases. Store in refrigerator.

Filling: Melt chocolate and cream in pan over low heat, do not boil. Remove from heat, cool 5 minutes, stir in butter and egg yolk with wooden spoon, add rum, beat until thick.

Note: To shell pistachio nuts, bring small pan of water to boil, add nuts, simmer 4 minutes; drain. Shell nuts and peel away brown skin.

Makes about 25.

SESAME NUT CARAMELS

1 cup sugar
90g butter
2 tablespoons golden syrup
⅓ cup liquid glucose
½ cup sweetened condensed milk
60g unsalted peanuts
¼ cup sesame seeds

Combine sugar, butter, golden syrup, glucose and condensed milk in pan, stir over low heat until sugar is dissolved. Increase heat, bring to boil; boil rapidly 7 minutes or until light golden brown, stirring constantly. Quickly stir in chopped peanuts, pour immediately into greased lamington tin (base measures 16cm × 26cm), cool until warm. Cut caramel mixture into three even strips lengthwise. Using hand, roll each strip on smooth surface to round off corners. Roll caramel rolls in toasted sesame seeds. Refrigerate until firm, cut into 1cm slices. Store in refrigerator.

Makes about 60.

To toast sesame seeds: Place sesame seeds in small pan, stir over low heat until golden brown. Remove from pan immediately.

Note: There is no substitute for liquid glucose in this recipe.

110

TOFFEE DIPPED GRAPES
2 cups sugar
1½ cups water
250g grapes
Wash and dry grapes, cut into small bunches. Make sure grapes are perfect and firmly attached to stems.

Combine sugar and water in pan, stir over heat until sugar is dissolved. Bring to boil, do not stir, boil rapidly for about 10 minutes or until toffee is light golden brown. Allow bubbles to subside, quickly dip grapes into toffee, use tongs to hold grapes, place on aluminium foil-covered tray to set.

Clockwise from top: Almond Rock Candy; Fruity Macaroon Log; Toffee Dipped Grapes.

FRUITY MACAROON LOG

A saddle tin is a fluted semi-circular cake tin available from cookware shops. However, a bar tin (base measures 7cm × 25cm) would be a good substitute.

185g dark cooking chocolate
125g red glace cherries
30g angelica or green glace cherries
30g sultanas
30g mixed peel
185g (2 cups) coconut
½ cup castor sugar
2 eggs
Line a saddle tin with aluminium foil so that it protrudes over each end of tin about 5cm. Chop chocolate roughly, sprinkle over base of tin; place in moderate oven few minutes or until just melted. Spread chocolate evenly over base of pan. Chop cherries and angelica, mix with sultanas and peel. Sprinkle fruit mixture evenly down the centre of the chocolate.

Mix coconut and sugar with eggs, distribute evenly over fruit mixture, level top. Bake in moderately hot oven 30 minutes or until lightly browned. Cool, refrigerate overnight, turn out, store wrapped in aluminium foil in refrigerator. Serve thin slices.

ALMOND ROCK CANDY
1 cup sugar
250g butter
60g blanched almonds
250g dark cooking chocolate
90g flaked almonds
Combine butter and sugar in thick-based pan, stir constantly over medium heat until mixture begins to boil. Boil without stirring for about 5 minutes or until golden brown. Add coarsely chopped blanched almonds and boil further 5 minutes or until hard crack stage (150 degrees C on sweets thermometer). Spread evenly in aluminium foil-lined lamington tin (base measures 16cm × 26cm) allow to cool and set. Melt chocolate over hot water. Remove caramel from tin, spread half the chocolate on one side, sprinkle with half the chopped flaked almonds. Refrigerate until set, then spread other side with remaining chocolate and almonds. When set, cut or break into small pieces.

Homemade liqueurs make great gifts for friends; make them about 3 months before giving them away.

LIQUEURS

COFFEE LIQUEUR
1 cup sugar
1 tablespoon instant coffee powder
1 cup water
2 teaspoons vanilla
1 cup brandy
1½ tablespoons rum
Combine sugar, coffee and water in pan, stir over heat until sugar is dissolved. Bring to boil, reduce heat, simmer uncovered for 3 minutes. Remove from heat, cool to lukewarm, add vanilla, brandy and rum. Pour into sterilised bottle or jar, seal, store in cool dark place for 2 weeks.

Makes about 2 cups.

STRAWBERRY LIQUEUR
2 punnets (500g) strawberries
2 cups gin
1 cup sugar
Wash and hull strawberries, cut in half, place in china or plastic container with gin, cover tightly, stand 2 days. Add sugar, stir to dissolve, strain; pour into sterilised bottle or jar, seal, stand in cool dark place for at least 2 weeks.

Makes about 2½ cups.

CHOCOLATE CREAM LIQUEUR
400g can sweetened condensed milk
300ml carton cream
3 eggs
1 cup whisky
1½ tablespoons bottled chocolate topping
¼ teaspoon coconut essence
Blend or process all ingredients together. Pour into sterilised bottle or jar, seal, store in cool dark place. This drink does not require refrigeration or keeping time for flavors to develop.

Makes about 4 cups.

CUMQUAT LIQUEUR

Eat the cumquats after drinking the liqueur — they are delicious with cream or ice cream.

500g cumquats
2 cups sugar
750ml bottle brandy
Wash cumquats, prick well with darning needle. Combine all ingredients in large sterilised jar fitted with plastic lid. Reverse jar each day to dissolve sugar. Do this for 4 weeks. Strain into sterilised bottle or jar, seal, store in cool dark place.

Makes about 3 cups.

Clockwise from bottom left: Strawberry Liqueur; Coffee Liqueur; Cumquat Liqueur; Chocolate Cream Liqueur.

PUNCHES

We've chosen 6 of our favorite punches, 3 alcoholic and 3 non alcoholic. Remember to have all ingredients well chilled, and add any sparkling aerated drinks just before serving. If the punch has to stand a long time serve ice separately, as it dilutes the drink too much.

MINTED LIME PUNCH
1 lime or lemon
mint leaves
1 cup bottled Lemon and Lime
   Barley Water
1.25 litre bottle Club Soda Squash
1.25 litre bottle soda water

Set some whole mint leaves in ice cubes to use in the punch just before serving. Slice lime or lemon thinly. Combine chilled barley water, Soda Squash and lemon slices, add chilled soda water just before serving; add mint ice cubes.

Makes about 2¾ litres.

COCONUT PINEAPPLE PUNCH
420g can coconut cream
½ cup vodka
3 cups canned pineapple juice
1 tablespoon icing sugar
2 tablespoons creme de menthe

Combine coconut cream, vodka, pineapple juice, icing sugar and creme de menthe in large bowl, mix well. Refrigerate before serving.

Makes 1½ litres.

STRAWBERRY CHAMPAGNE PUNCH
3 punnets strawberries
⅔ cup icing sugar
⅓ cup Grand Marnier
2 tablespoons lemon juice
2 x 750ml bottles champagne

Hull strawberries. Place 2½ punnets of strawberries in blender or processor; add icing sugar, Grand Marnier and lemon juice, blend on high speed until pureed. Place strawberry mixture in punch bowl; just before serving, add cold champagne and remaining chopped strawberries.

Makes 2½ litres.

PINEAPPLE TEA PUNCH
1 ripe pineapple
2 cups cold black tea
12 mint leaves
2 x 285ml bottles dry ginger ale

Peel pineapple, remove core, chop pineapple roughly. Place half the chopped pineapple, 1 cup of the black tea and mint leaves into blender or processor; blend on high speed 30 seconds or until pineapple is finely crushed.

Repeat with remaining pineapple and black tea. Refrigerate pineapple mixture until cold. Just before serving, top with chilled ginger ale.

Makes about 1½ litres.

FRUIT PUNCH
450g can crushed pineapple
3 passionfruit
1 cup lemon juice (approximately 5 lemons)
2 cups orange juice (approximately 6 oranges)
500ml bottle soda water
1 tablespoon sugar

Combine undrained pineapple, passionfruit pulp, lemon and orange juices and sugar in large bowl or jug, refrigerate until well chilled. Just before serving add chilled soda water, stir to combine.

Makes about 1½ litres.

FRUIT SHERRY PUNCH
1 cup orange juice
1 cup apple juice
¾ cup dry sherry
500ml bottle ginger ale
500ml bottle soda water
1 lemon
½ cucumber
1 tablespoon chopped mint

Combine orange juice, apple juice, sherry, finely sliced lemon and cucumber; mix well; refrigerate. Just before serving, add chilled ginger ale, soda water and mint.

Makes about 1¾ litres.

Back row, from left: Minted Lime, Pineapple Tea, Strawberry Champagne and Coconut Pineapple Punches. Front row: Fruit Punch and Fruit Sherry Punch.

Choose unblemished, slightly under-ripe fruit for jams and jellies. Use a large pan or boiler to allow maximum evaporation of liquid in minimum time. Once the sugar has been added, do not have the mixture deeper than 5cm; if it is, dissolve the sugar, then cook the jam mixture in batches. Cooking times given are only a guide; when the mixture will fall from a wooden spoon in heavy drops, remove jam from heat, allow bubbles to subside, then drop a teaspoon of jam onto a cold saucer; when cold it is easy to tell if the jam is ready or not.

WHISKY SEVILLE MARMALADE

This is like the true bitter English marmalade. Seville oranges are available in winter; any other type of orange can be used.

1kg Seville oranges (4 large)
2 litres water
2½kg sugar, approximately
3 tablespoons whisky

Wash oranges, slice very finely, reserve seeds. Place fruit in basin, add water, cover, stand overnight. Place seeds in cup, cover with extra water, cover, stand overnight.

Next day, place fruit mixture in large boiler, strain seeds, add this liquid to fruit mixture, press as much liquid as possible from seeds into fruit mixture; discard seeds. Cover boiler, bring mixture to boil, reduce heat, simmer, covered about 1 hour, or until fruit rind is tender. Measure fruit mixture, allow one cup sugar to each one cup of fruit mixture. Return fruit mixture and sugar to boiler, stir without boiling over high heat until sugar is dissolved. Bring to boil, boil as rapidly as possible uncovered without stirring, 30 to 40 minutes or until jam will jell on a cold saucer.

Stand 5 minutes, stir in whisky, pour into hot sterilised jars and seal when cold.

Makes about 10 cups.

PRESERVES

These jams and jellies are easy to make and perfect for gifts.

APPLE AND ROSE WINE JELLY
1kg Granny Smith apples (about 5 large)
1 lemon
1½ litres water
1 cup rosé wine
1½kg sugar, approximately

Wash fruit, chop unpeeled apples and lemon roughly, place in large boiler with water, cover, bring to boil, reduce heat, simmer covered 1 hour, or until fruit is pulpy. Add wine, cover, simmer further 30 minutes. Strain mixture through fine, well wrung-out damp cloth, allow mixture to drip through cloth overnight, do not squeeze or press mixture through cloth; this gives a cloudy jelly.

Next day, discard fruit mixture, measure liquid, allow 1 cup sugar to each one cup of liquid. Combine liquid and sugar in boiler, stir over high heat without boiling until sugar is dissolved. Bring to boil, do not stir, boil as rapidly as possible uncovered for 10 to 15 minutes, or until mixture will jell when tested on a cold saucer. Pour mixture into hot sterilised jars, seal when cold.

Makes about 6 cups.

MANDARIN MARNIER MARMALADE
1kg mandarins (about 16 small)
2 litres water
2kg sugar, approximately
3 tablespoons Grand Marnier

Wash fruit, slice as finely as possible, reserve seeds. Place seeds in small basin, cover with a little extra water, stand overnight. Place sliced fruit and water in separate basin, cover, stand overnight.

Next day, strain seeds, reserve liquid, use spoon to press as much liquid as possible from seeds, discard seeds, place liquid in large boiler with fruit mixture. Cover, bring to boil, reduce heat, simmer, covered, 45 to 60 minutes or until rind is tender.

Measure fruit mixture and allow one cup sugar to each cup of fruit mixture. Return fruit mixture to boiler with sugar. Stir jam constantly over high heat without boiling until sugar is dissolved. Bring to boil, boil rapidly uncovered without stirring until jam will jell when tested on a cold saucer; this will take 30 to 40 minutes.

Stand 5 minutes, stir in Grand Marnier, pour into hot sterilised jars, seal when cold.

Makes about 9 cups.

APRICOT RUM CONSERVE
500g dried apricots
1 litre water
⅓ cup lemon juice
1kg sugar
2 tablespoons rum

Combine apricots, water and strained lemon juice in pan, cover, bring to boil, reduce heat, simmer covered 30 minutes, or until apricots are tender. Add sugar, stir without boiling over high heat until sugar is dissolved. Bring to boil, boil rapidly uncovered, without stirring, for about 15 minutes or until mixture is thick and will drop heavily from spoon; check by allowing a spoonful to set on a cold saucer. Allow bubbles to subside, stir in rum, pour into hot sterilised jars and seal when cold.

Makes about 6 cups.

BERRY JAM WITH KIRSCH

Any berries can be used — raspberries, strawberries, loganberries, blackberries and so on. We used an equal combination of raspberries and blackberries.

1kg fresh or frozen berries
1kg sugar
1 cup lemon juice (3 to 4 lemons)
3 tablespoons kirsch

Combine berries, sugar and strained lemon juice in large pan, stir over medium heat without boiling until sugar is dissolved. Bring to boil, do not stir, boil uncovered as rapidly as possible for about 15 minutes or until jam will jell on a cold saucer.

Stir in kirsch, pour into hot sterilised jars, seal when cold.

Makes about 5 cups.

Dress up your preserves with gingham covers, a pretty bow and your own labels.

ROSE PETAL JELLY

Commercial pectin is necessary for this recipe; it is available from health food stores and stores which sell home preserving equipment. There are several brands available; if using Jamsetta, 2 tablespoons of the pectin are required; Citrus Pectin, made by Hunza, is more concentrated and requires only 1 teaspoon to set the jelly. Be sure to use rose petals which have not been sprayed with pesticides.

125g red rose petals (about 15 large roses)
3 cups water
¼ cup lemon juice
2 cups sugar, approximately
commercial pectin

Pull petals from roses, cut away any tough pieces at base of petals with scissors, place petals in strainer, rinse gently under cold running water; drain well. Place petals in large pan, add water and lemon juice, bring to boil, reduce heat; simmer covered 30 minutes. Strain through fine damp cloth, do not force liquid through cloth. Measure liquid, allow ¾ cup sugar to each 1 cup of liquid. Return liquid and sugar to pan. Stir over heat without boiling, until sugar is dissolved.

Bring to boil, do not stir, boil rapidly uncovered for 15 minutes. Add pectin, stir until dissolved, boil further 3 minutes. Pour into hot sterilised jars, seal when cold.

Makes 2 cups.

BLACK GRAPE AND PORT JELLY
1kg black grapes
2 lemons
1 litre water
½ cup port
1kg sugar, approximately

Wash fruit, remove grapes from stalks, discard stalks. Combine grapes, roughly chopped lemons and water in large boiler, cover, bring to boil, reduce heat, simmer 45 minutes. Add port; use potato masher to crush grapes, cover, simmer further 45 minutes. Strain mixture through fine, well wrung-out damp cloth; allow mixture to drip through cloth overnight, do not squeeze or press mixture through cloth; this will give a cloudy jelly.

Next day, discard fruit mixture, measure liquid, allow ¾ cup sugar to each one cup of liquid. Combine liquid and sugar in boiler, stir over high heat without boiling until sugar is dissolved. Bring to boil, do not stir, boil as rapidly as possible uncovered for about 15 minutes, or until mixture will jell when tested on a cold saucer. Pour mixture into hot sterilised jars, seal when cold.

Makes about 4 cups.

BRANDIED LIME MARMALADE

Some limes are seedless — they are fine for this recipe. Limes are so rich in pectin they do not need help from the extra pectin in the seeds.

1kg limes (about 12 medium)
2 litres water
2kg sugar, approximately
½ cup brandy

Wash limes, slice as finely as possible, discard seeds. Place limes in basin with water, cover, stand overnight. Next day, place lime mixture in boiler, cover, bring to boil, reduce heat, simmer covered 1 hour or until rind is tender. Measure mixture; allow one cup sugar to each one cup of mixture. Return lime mixture and sugar to boiler, stir over high heat without boiling until sugar is dissolved.

Bring to boil, boil as rapidly as possible without stirring for 20 minutes or until jam will jell when tested on a cold saucer.

Stand 5 minutes, stir in brandy, pour into hot sterilised jars and seal when cold.

Makes about 9 cups.

STRAWBERRY LIQUEUR CONSERVE

This jam does not jell like a marmalade, with fruit suspended in a jelly. It should set to a soft, spreadable consistency.

LIQUEUR
2 x 250g punnets strawberries
½ cup sugar
½ cup gin
CONSERVE
250g punnet strawberries
1 cup sugar
2 teaspoons grated lemon rind
2 tablespoons lemon juice

Hull strawberries, combine in jar with sugar and gin, cover, stand 3 days. Shake or gently stir strawberries several times to dissolve sugar, strain. (Liquid can be served as a liqueur or as a dessert sauce; it is not used in the conserve.) Reserve strawberries, to add to the conserve.

Conserve: Hull strawberries, place in pan with sugar, lemon rind, lemon juice and reserved strawberries from liqueur. Stir gently over heat without boiling until sugar is dissolved. Bring to boil, do not stir, boil uncovered for about 10 minutes, or until mixture will set to a spreading consistency when cooled on a cold saucer. Pour into hot sterilized jars, seal when cold.

Makes about 2 cups.

CUMQUAT COINTREAU JAM
1kg cumquats
(about 60 small)
1½ litres water
1½kg sugar, approximately
3 tablespoons Cointreau

Wash fruit, cut into quarters or eighths, depending on size of fruit; remove seeds, place seeds in small basin, cover with a little extra water, stand overnight. Combine fruit with water in basin, cover, stand overnight. Next day, place fruit mixture in boiler; strain seeds, place liquid into boiler, press as much liquid as possible from seeds into boiler, discard seeds. Bring to boil, reduce heat, simmer covered 45 to 60 minutes or until rind is tender. Measure mixture, allow one cup of sugar to each one cup of mixture, return fruit mixture and sugar to boiler, stir over high heat without boiling until sugar is dissolved.

Bring to boil without stirring, boil uncovered as rapidly as possible for 25 to 35 minutes, or until mixture will jell when tested on a cold saucer.

Stand 5 minutes, stir in Cointreau, pour into hot sterilised jars and seal when cold.

Makes about 6 cups.

CHILLI ONIONS

Onions can be eaten a few days after pickling but they are better left for four weeks. They will darken on standing.

2kg small pickling onions
750g cooking salt
5 cups white vinegar
4 teaspoons cooking salt, extra
1 tablespoon sugar
1½ teaspoons whole cloves
2 teaspoons whole allspice
2 teaspoons whole black peppercorns
½ teaspoon chilli powder
15 cloves garlic (about 2 knobs)
20 small red chillies

Place unpeeled onions and 750g salt in large bowl, add enough water to cover, stand two days, stirring occasionally. Strain, peel onions, leaving ends intact so onions do not fall apart during the pickling process.

Place in bowl, cover with boiling water, stand 3 minutes, drain. Repeat this process twice. After draining the onions well for the third time, pack into sterilised jars.

Peel garlic, leave whole. Remove stems from chillies, leave chillies whole. Combine garlic and chillies in pan with remaining ingredients. Bring to boil, reduce heat, simmer uncovered 15 minutes, cool slightly then pour equal amounts of garlic and chillies over onions; seal when cold.

PICKLED CHILLIES
500g large chillies
⅓ cup cooking salt
3 cups water
3 cups white vinegar
1 tablespoon cooking salt, extra
2 tablespoons whole black peppercorns

Wash chillies, cut stalks from chillies, cut away any bruised or marked parts of chillies, do not remove seeds. Place chillies, salt and water in basin, stir until salt is dissolved, cover, stand 24 hours. Drain, rinse well under cold water. Pack chillies into hot sterilised jars. Combine vinegar, extra salt and peppercorns in pan, bring to boil, reduce heat, cover, simmer 5 minutes, remove from heat, stand 5 minutes.

Pour over chillies, seal when cold. Store for 6 weeks before using.

BREAD AND BUTTER CUCUMBERS
4 large cucumbers
cooking salt
1½ cups white vinegar
1 cup water
¾ cup sugar
2 teaspoons mustard seeds
½ small red pepper

Wash cucumbers, slice thinly. Place

Homemade preserves are a great way to use cheap vegetables or when your garden gives you a bumper crop.

cucumber slices in layers in large shallow dish, sprinkling a little salt between each layer. (You will need about ¼ cup salt.) Cover, stand overnight. Rinse cucumbers well under cold water, drain. Combine vinegar, water, sugar, mustard seeds, one teaspoon salt in pan, stir until sugar is dissolved, bring to boil, reduce heat, simmer uncovered five minutes. Add cucumbers, bring to boil, remove from heat.

Using tongs and working quickly, pack cucumbers tightly into hot, sterilised jars. Add a few thin strips of red pepper to each jar. Fill with vinegar mixture to within 1cm of top, seal when cold.

FRUIT CHUTNEY
6 tomatoes
3 large onions
3 Granny Smith apples
4 cups brown vinegar
500g brown sugar
1 cup sultanas
½ cup currants
1 teaspoon cinnamon
1½ teaspoons dry mustard
½ teaspoon ground cloves
¼ teaspoon cayenne
1 tablespoon cooking salt
¼ cup tomato paste

Peel tomatoes, chop roughly, chop onions; peel, core and chop apples. Combine all ingredients in large pan or boiler, stir over heat until sugar is dissolved. Bring to boil, reduce heat, simmer uncovered approximately 2½ hours or until chutney is thick. Chutney will need to be stirred occasionally toward the end of the cooking time. Pour into hot sterilised jars, cool, seal.

Makes about 5 cups.

MUSTARD CHOKO PICKLES
4 chokos
2 large onions
2 tablespoons cooking salt
1 cup water
⅓ cup plain flour
2 tablespoons dry mustard
1 teaspoon turmeric
½ teaspoon ground cloves
1 cup sugar
½ cup golden syrup
2 cups brown vinegar

Peel chokos, cut into 1cm pieces; cut onions into 1cm pieces. Combine chokos, onions and salt in bowl, stand covered overnight. Drain, rinse well under cold water. Place choko mixture in pan with water, bring to boil, reduce heat, simmer covered 15 minutes. Blend flour, mustard, turmeric, cloves and sugar with vinegar and golden syrup. Add to choko mixture, stir until boiling, reduce heat, simmer uncovered 30 minutes or until mixture is thick. Pour into hot sterilised jars, seal when cold.

Makes about 6 cups.

GIFTS

Two gift ideas for Christmas and two for any other time to give your friends and family. These are suitable for children to make; perhaps the Christmas tree would need adult supervision.

CHOCOLATE HAZELNUT CHRISTMAS TREE

This tree takes a little time to make, but it is delightful to look at and delicious to eat. The Christmas Tree can be made some days in advance. If the weather is hot, keep it refrigerated.

500g dark chocolate (see note at end of recipe)
250g roasted hazelnuts
1 brazil nut
60g dark chocolate, extra
2 teaspoons icing sugar

Roughly chop chocolate, place in top half of double saucepan, place over gently simmering water; make sure water does not touch base of top saucepan. When chocolate is completely melted and smooth, remove from heat and water, stir in roughly chopped hazelnuts; mix well.

Note: Do not use blender or food processor for chopping nuts, they will be chopped too finely.

While chocolate is melting, prepare trays for making branches of tree. Cover trays with a piece of aluminium foil; any flat tray, upturned cake tin, base of baking dish, or pieces of

heavy cardboard can be used. It is important the surface be level and rigid enough so the branches do not bend while they are setting. Bread boards or pieces of wood covered with foil can be used but the chocolate will take longer to set. We used three scone slides.

Mark nine crosses on the foil, leave about 2.5cm between each cross. The measurements for the crosses are: 7cm; 9cm; 11cm; 13cm; 14cm; 15cm; 16cm; 17cm; 18cm.

Prepare a base for the tree; you will need a piece of heavy cardboard or pressed hardboard 20cm in diameter, it must be rigid and strong enough to support all the branches of the tree. Cover with decorative silver paper or foil. Mark a cross 18cm on this base board. Using a teaspoon, drop teaspoonfuls of chocolate mixture along the marked crosses. Do the cross on the base board first, refrigerate, then do the remaining crosses in order of size, starting from the largest size and working to the smallest. Refrigerate crosses as soon as they are complete, for several hours or, if desired, overnight. Do not freeze.

Note: If kitchen is cool, chocolate can be left to set at room temperature; this will mean the tree will take longer to make, but chocolate will have more sheen than if it is refrigerated.

Melt extra chocolate over simmering water. To assemble tree, join the largest cross to the cross on the base board by dropping about a teaspoon of the melted chocolate into the centre of the cross on the base board; position the cross on top, as shown. It may be necessary to move the top cross around until the best position is found; if branches look a little uneven, support underneath with a match box.

Drop about half a teaspoon of the melted chocolate on top of the second cross; this forms a good base when adding the next pair of crosses.

Assemble the remaining eight crosses in pairs, starting from the largest remaining cross to the smallest cross, refrigerate until chocolate is set; about 15 minutes.

When each pair of crosses is set, place the largest pair on top of the crosses on the base board, joining with melted chocolate as before. It is important each section be completely set before topping with another pair of crosses.

When tree is assembled, cut an end off the brazil nut, so it will sit neatly on top of the tree, place in position with melted chocolate, cover nut with chocolate and then refrigerate until set. Dust tree lightly with sifted icing sugar.

Note: The dark cooking chocolate available from health food stores and packaged cooking chocolate available from supermarkets are ideal for making this tree. The compound chocolates, although less expensive, are not suitable.

MARASCHINO CHOCOLATE BELLS

Little chocolate bells are so appealing with a maraschino cherry hidden inside, and they are quite simple to make. A small bow adds a festive touch. Recipe makes about 30 chocolates.

1 packet 6 small Christmas bells (see note below)
250g packet dark cooking compound chocolate (see note below)
227g jar maraschino cherries

STEP 1
Wash and dry bells thoroughly. Melt chocolate over simmering water. Spread a little chocolate inside bell, use skewer to spread chocolate into top of bell shape. Place on plate, freeze for 2 minutes.

Note: The small plastic Christmas bells used were obtained from a chain store in packets of 6. Chocolate is available from most supermarkets.

STEP 2
Place a halved maraschino cherry, cut side up, inside bell. Spread with a little more melted chocolate to seal bell completely. Return to freezer for 5 minutes.

STEP 3
Using small, fine skewer, insert skewer into top part of bell, as shown. This will break the seal of the chocolate inside the bell, allowing it to be removed without difficulty.

Using skewer, drop a small amount of chocolate on top of each bell, place small ribbon bow in position. These bells will remain solid at room temperature.

COLORED SUGARS
These make such a pretty gift and are a novelty when put on the table, in their jars, to use with after-dinner coffee. White with two contrasting colors looks attractive. Coffee jars make good containers; if they have a glass lid with plastic seal, remove this, fill the lid with sugars, making sure they are firmly packed, then put the plastic seal back in position.

To color the sugar: Work with about 1 cup of sugar at a time. Use granulated (ordinary) sugar or coffee crystals. Do not use castor sugar: it is too fine. Put it into a plastic bag, add a drop or two of desired food coloring (depending on the density of color required), then shake and squeeze the bag until the coloring is evenly distributed through the sugar. Repeat for other colors.

To fill into jars: Put the sugars into small jugs, such as measuring jugs. Alternate the colors and white sugar, making geometric patterns. The handle of a teaspoon or a paint brush will help push the sugar up the sides of the jar to make fancy patterns, as desired.

Make sure jar is tightly packed so that the pattern will not move and change shape; press sugar down firmly with palm of hand or back of spoon when jar is full. Top up with more sugar if necessary.

DOUGH BASKETS

Dough can be used to make an excellent fruit or bread basket. The dough can be made into many other shapes: any number of cutouts can be created.

4 cups plain flour
1½ cups salt (see note below)
1½ cups water, approximately
1 egg yolk
2 tablespoons water, extra

Sift flour and salt into basin, mix well with fingertips. Make well in centre, add water, mix with knife; when ingredients become too stiff to stir, use hand to combine ingredients, a little extra water may be needed to make dough firm but pliable. Turn onto lightly floured surface, knead until smooth. If dough is at the correct consistency, it will not be necessary to use any more flour for handling or kneading the dough.

Cover a flat scone tray with a piece of aluminium foil. Grease outside of an upturned loaf tin lightly but evenly. Place tin in freezer or refrigerator for few minutes, or until greasing is set. Place on tray upside down. Take small handfuls of dough, work with fingers until smooth, then roll to sausage shape about the thickness of your fingers, lay rolls crossways over tin, as shown. It doesn't matter how thick the rolls are, or how many there are, but it is important that there be an uneven number across the tin. Leave rolls about 2.5cm longer than the width of the tin, as shown.

Make rolls to go lengthways over the tin. Lift every second cross roll and place the long rolls in position, weaving the rolls of dough, as shown.

Make a roll long enough to go right around the sides of the tin, or make two rolls; they can be joined, as shown. Weave the roll over and under the other rolls, as before. Make sure the joins meet under a roll of dough so the joins will be hidden. Use combined egg yolk and extra water to join pieces of dough together.

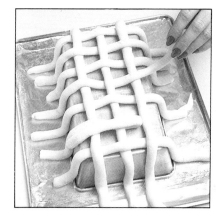

Above: Weave rolls of dough over and under for basket weave effect.
Below: Place twisted rolls of dough around tin for plaited edge.

Roll two long sausage shapes of dough to same thickness as before and twist to form a rope edging for basket; do not stretch the dough.

Cut off ends of criss-crossed rolls at an angle against tin, brush with combined egg yolk and water, press rope edging into position over cut ends. Rope edging can be made in one long piece, or can be joined neatly, using egg glazing. Glaze the whole basket as evenly as possible with egg glazing, bake in very slow oven for about 4 hours. Time will depend on thickness of dough.

Glaze basket once or twice more during the cooking time for a richer color. Turn oven off, leave basket to become cold in the oven; when cold, remove from tin. If dough does not feel completely dried out, return basket to very slow oven without the tin for another hour or two. It is important the dough be dry before varnishing or the basket will develop mould. Brush basket completely with clear varnish or lacquer, leave to dry, preferably overnight. Another coat of varnish will give an even better appearance to the basket.

Note: Use only coarse cooking salt (common salt) for making this dough; do not use fine table salt.

Note: If using ovenproof glass bowls to shape the baskets, remove the bowls halfway through cooking time to allow the baskets to dry out.

INDEX